Techn(

Borut Rončević and Victor Cepoi (eds.)

Technologies and Innovations in Regional Development: The European Union and its Strategies

PETER LANG

Bibliographic Information published by the Deutsche Nationalbibliothek
The Deutsche Nationalbibliothek lists this publication in the Deutsche Nationalbibliografie; detailed bibliographic data is available online at http://dnb.d-nb.de.

Library of Congress Cataloging-in-Publication Data
A CIP catalog record for this book has been applied for at the Library of Congress.

This publication was financially co-funded by the Erasmus+ programme of the European Union, Key Action: Erasmus+, Jean Monnet, Action Type: Jean Monnet Centre of Excellence, Project Reference: 587540-EPP-1-2017-1-SIEPPJMO-CoE

Co-funded by the Erasmus+ Programme of the European Union

Jean Monnet Centre of Excellence
TIR 2020

More information on TIR 2020 project available at https://www.tir2020.net/

ISBN 978-3-631-83806-8 (Print)
E-ISBN 978-3-631-83890-7 (E-PDF)
E-ISBN 978-3-631-83891-4 (EPUB)
DOI: 10.3726/b17733

PETER LANG Open

Peter Lang · Berlin · Bern · Bruxelles · Istanbul · New York · Oxford · Warszawa · Wien

This publication has been peer reviewed.

www.peterlang.com

Table of Contents

List of Contributors

Tamara Besednjak Valič
Faculty of Information Studies in Novo mesto, Slovenia
tamara.valic@fis.unm.si

Victor Cepoi
Faculty of Information Studies in Novo mesto, Slovenia
victor.cepoi@fis.unm.si

Urška Fric
Faculty of Information Studies in Novo mesto
urska.fric@fis.unm.si

Cristian Gangaliuc
Faculty of Information Studies in Novo mesto, Slovenia
cristian.gangaliuc@fis.unm.si

Tea Golob
School of Advanced Social Studies, Slovenia
tea.golob@fuds.si

Petra Kleindienst
School of Advanced Social Studies, Slovenia
petra.kleindiest.@fuds.si

Dolores Modic
Nord University, Norway
dolores.modic@nord.no

Alenka Pandiloska Jurak
Faculty of Information Studies in Novo mesto, Slovenia
alenka.pandiloska@fis.unm.si

Borut Rončević
Faculty of Information Studies, Slovenia
borut.roncevic@fis.unm.si

Borut Rončević, Dolores Modic, and Tea Golob

Social-Fields-Approach (SOFIA) to Research on Social Change: Innovations as Social Fields

Abstract: This chapter introduces the Social-Fields-Approach (SOFIA) to research on social change. This is an approach to conceptualisation and operationalization for the purpose of empirical exploration. In SOFIA, we understand the empirical reality as a social field shaped by the three social forces: institutions, social networks, and cognitive frames. Social fields and the social forces are conceptualised and operationalised in line with theoretical background and specific research questions for the purpose of qualitative, quantitative, and mixed methods research.

In this chapter we first examine the theoretical background of the approach and provide the relevant literature review. We continue by outlining the approach. This is followed by elucidating SOFIA by applying it to innovation systems. We conclude by deliberating on the promise of the approach, carefully considering the challenges and dilemmas, and pondering over the potential of this approach for the future.

Keywords: Social-Fields-Approach, operationalisation, innovations, institutions, social networks, cognitive frames

1. Introduction

The ancient Greek philosopher Heraclitus famously stated that the only constant in life is change. Ibn Khaldun's *Muqaddimah*, written in 1377, perhaps the first work in the field of social sciences, attempts to unveil a pattern of historic changes in social organisations. Saint-Simone discussed 'social physiology', the processes running inside society, at the beginning of the 19th century, and Auguste Comte, the first to publish the term 'sociology', dedicated significant attention to 'social dynamics' in addition to 'social statics'.

While the simplistic organic metaphor, specifically the classic approach to social change (Sztompka, 1994), was relatively early superseded by more complex and nuanced approaches, social change has always been in the minds of scholars. Modern social research is, to a significant extent, an intellectual response to the need to understand ambiguities, complexities, and new realities caused by the unprecedented transformations in all areas of social life, a result of technological and socio-economic changes caused by the industrial revolution.

The organic approach differentiating the static and the dynamic evolved into the systems model, in which social change 'is conceived as the change occurring within, or embracing the social system' (Sztompka, 1994: 4), which was superseded by the dynamic social field model of social change, in which a certain social entity or phenomenon is no longer considered as an 'object', but as a 'continuous, unending stream of events' (Sztompka, 1994: 9), which implies that social reality is dynamic from the perspective of a social researcher.

The concept of social fields has been recognised as being able to explain how stability and change are achieved by social actors in circumscribed social settings (Fligstein and McAdam, 2011). The key contribution of the ideas related to social fields is in shifting focus to the fact that changes within a field are induced by both a person's 'own motion through the field and by internal developments of the field itself' (Martin, 2003: 18) as well as in recognising the existence of the mutual interdependence of coexisting facts, which are forming a particular field (Lewin, 1951). Social fields were able to inform a range of research, from cultural (e.g., McNay, 1999; Golob and Makarovič, 2018), political (e.g., Turner, 1974; Lubbers et al., 2020), and economic (e.g., Hannan and Freeman, 1984; Beckert, 2010) studies, and more recently, studies of innovation (e.g., Rončević and Modic, 2011; Cepoi and Golob, 2017; Cepoi, 2019).

The *Social-Fields-Approach (SOFIA)* is an approach to conceptualisation and operationalisation for the purpose of empirical research, in which we employ Jens Beckert's (2010) variant of social fields theory that understands empirical reality as a social field shaped by the three social forces: institutions, social networks, and cognitive frames. While Beckert used this approach to analyse markets as social fields, SOFIA can also be used as an approach for the analysis of other social fields. One example is the conceptualisation of regional innovation systems as social fields shaped by the aforementioned social forces. We first employed this approach in 2011, only a year after Beckert's (2010) seminal work, by applying SOFIA in our secondary analysis of technological innovation in seven regions on four continents (Rončević and Modic, 2011). This approach was further refined in subsequent publications (Rončević and Modic, 2011; Rončević, 2012; Rončević and Modic, 2012; Rončević et al., 2018), gradually increasing the empirical base and introducing new sources of secondary data. This change allowed for more fine-grained analysis and revelation of the nuanced impact of individual forces and, most importantly, the relevance of their combined influence on the structuration of regional innovation systems (Modic and Rončević, 2018). However, the approach was not limited to the research of regional innovation systems but is also used for researching other levels of innovation systems (e.g., Cepoi and Golob, 2017), specifically other spatial levels. Lastly, this volume will point to other possible future applications of SOFIA. Since 2017, we have been developing SOFIA in the framework of the Jean Monnet Centre of Excellence 'Technologies and Innovations in Regional Development for Europe 2020', where this was the theoretical and conceptual background in which we developed operationalisation for the purpose of primary data collection in empirical research for the first time. Noteworthily, on this basis, the Centre of Excellence has collected data from 21 European regions.

As a result, SOFIA is now at the level at which it provides possibilities for both primary and secondary research and also to expand to research on other phenomena. The approach is appropriate for most, if not all, possible research methods and sample sizes. We can use it for quantitative, qualitative, and mixed-method studies (e.g., qualitative comparative analysis QCA), and even in computer modelling (see Džajić Uršič, 2020). SOFIA can be used in large-N and small-N samples, as well as in single case studies. Furthermore, we can use it not only for basic but also for applied research. Thus far, it has been effectively utilised in four international EU-funded applied projects.[1]

In this chapter, we elaborate on the application of SOFIA in sociological research on innovation to showcase how one can explore complex phenomena, which require specific conceptualisation and operationalisation, on different spatial (e.g., national, regional, local), social (micro, meso, macro) and sectoral levels. In particular, we link the phenomena of the three social forces to the innovation systems literature. Furthermore, we show that SOFIA enables tackling the mutual influence of social forces in innovation and allows for a more complex and nuanced understanding.

The chapter proceeds as follows. We first explicate the roots of the social fields theory. It is a theoretical background that allows us to study innovation processes and elucidate on the innovation activities and innovative society. Next, we provide an overview of the relevant literature on social structures, relevant to the explanation of economic outcomes. Three relevant social structures, i.e. social forces, have been identified (Fligstein and Dauter, 2007; Beckert,

1 These projects are High-performance Computing for Effective Innovation in the Danube Region (InnoHPC, 2017–2019, Danube Transnational Programme), Fostering Innovation in the Danube Region through Knowledge Engineering and IPR Management (KnowING IPR, 2018–2021, Danube Transnational Programme), Enabling SMEs to gain competitive advantage from the use of HPC (SME/HPC, 2017–2020, Erasmus+ Knowledge Alliances) and Labs of Innovation and Business for Young Actors of Start Up (Libya UP, 2019–2022, Erasmus+ Capacity Building in Higher Education).

2010; Modic and Rončević, 2011) and empirically confirmed (e.g., Modic and Rončević, 2018): social networks, institutions, and cognitive frames. In the following section, we explore these social forces in connection to the different spatial levels, using and connecting with the innovation systems framework (with elaboration on both so-called spatial and a-spatial innovation systems). We conclude this chapter by reiterating the purpose of this volume in terms of SOFIA and providing a guidepost through the rest of this volume. Thus, the chapter concludes by deliberating on the promise of the approach, carefully considering the challenges and dilemmas and pondering over the potential of this approach for the future.

2. The Theory of Social Fields and Its Roots

In this section, we describe the foundations of the social field theory and its key theoretical inspirations. Special attention is paid to the structural settings and possibilities for collective action within particular fields, which can elucidate the potential for innovations and their actual emergence. To approach the social fields as systems of innovation, we lean on the ideas of strategic action fields (cf. Fligstein and McAdam, 2012), which enable explaining how social actors achieve stability and change.

The notion of a *field* is nowadays widely associated with social phenomena, yet its roots go back to physical science. The concept of fields in social sciences derived from the ideas of a field as the emergent and dynamic reality in the realm of natural science (Wilkinson, 1970). Hence, the origins of the social field theory have quite a long history, and its inspirations can be found already in the Newtonian gravitation and ideas of electromagnetism. However, the theoretic form framing subsequent considerations of social fields ensues from Einstein's theory of general relativity (Hesse, 1970: 226; Martin, 2003; Martin and Gregg, 2015).

Martin (2003) has distinguished between three main streams of theoretical directions within the social sciences based on considerations and concepts from natural science. The first one ensues from the social-psychological Gestalt perspectives associated most notably with Lewin (1951), the second stream refers to the field theory of domination, competing positions, and unequal distribution of capital, associated with Bourdieu (1977), and the third stream refers to the theory of inter-organisation relations associated most notably with DiMaggio and Powel (1983).

According to Martin (2003), the ideas of *social field* initially emerged from the totalistic Gestalt theories, which argued that individuals had to be considered in relation to a wider perceptual field (see Martin, 2003: 16–18). The crucial contribution of such ideas for social sciences can be found in recognising the mutual interdependence of coexisting facts, which form a particular field (Lewin, 1951: 204). The relation between actor and structures of the fields imply an interrelation making a life-world inheritably affective. The person within a field has certain agential abilities asserting that she/he is able to move freely about in the field, while movement is a directed action and not just locomotion (Martin, 2003: 18). Changes within a field are induced by both a person's 'own motion through the field and by internal developments of the field itself' (ibid.)

The Gestalt tradition also inspired a branch of field theory, which Martin (2003) calls a conception of organised striving. As he explains, the concept originates from work elaborated by Max Weber, who recognised the idea of 'spheres of value' (Weber, 1915, 1964). The latter implies that spheres of values exist of some social logic referring to social fields held by actors and not because of some transcendent nature of human action (see Martin, 2003: 20). The most notable contributions in that regard were made by Pierre Bourdieu (1977, 1990), whose work on social fields remains highly influential. He was interested in the relationship between structure and the way people construct social reality. Bourdieu conceptualised practice as the effect of habitual schemes and dispositions (habitus), combined with resources (capital), all of which are constrained and activated through the structures, conditions and arrangements of objects in social space and social time (field).

The conception of institutional fields originates in ideas suggested by Mannheim (1940), describing 'the case of interdependent actions that transcend organisations or groups (sector fields)' (in Martin, 2003: 26). In that light, a field structure can emerge when units come into interaction. However, interactions are not just arbitrary ones. They need to induce a development of mutual influence, which is irreducible to existing institutional channels. Further, units of the field also align due to having similar goals (cf. Cooley, 1913 in Martin, 2003: 26). Mannheim's idea was adopted by Ronald Warren (1967), who focused on the field as something that explained trans-organisational consistencies. Interweaving the idea of field with a social organisation has also been elaborated by Wilkinson (1970), who approached a social field within a frame of interactional theory. In that light, a social field is argued to have a distinct existence, although recognising a certain role of ecological, cultural and psychological factors.

Following Manheim, DiMaggio and Powel (1983, 1991) connected the perspective of inter-relation organisations to Bourdieu's thinking (Martin, 2003: 27). DiMaggio and Powel (1991) define the concept organisational fields as comprising 'those organizations that, in aggregate, constitute a recognized area of institutional life: key suppliers, resource and product consumers, regulatory agencies, and other organizations that produce similar services or products' (1991: 64). As Martin argues (2003: 27), they exceeded simple suggestion referring to the idea that a field brings to the existence of elements within it to become situated in some way. Conversely, they suggested the structuration of the field is largely a result of patterns of relations. Furthermore, they emphasised that 'field position can empirically be specified by a close study of the ensemble of interpersonal relations' (Martin, 2003: 27).

In recent decades, interest in the concept of social fields has proliferated. According to Fligstein (2001, 2008), there has been an increased interest across various 'new institutional theories' which intend to explain 'how social institutions, defined as rules that produce social interaction, come into existence, remain stable, and are transformed' (2001: 230). They focus on the construction of local social orders, which could be called 'fields', 'arenas', or 'games', and problematise the relationship between actors and the social structures in which they are embedded. However, it has been argued that new institutionalisms have certain limitations referring to conceptualisations, which see fields as interactions between more and less powerful collective groups while taking into account shared meanings and rules. To overcome those limitations, a more social, collective conception of action is needed (ibid.).

Fligstein has developed a view of action called 'social skill', which originates in symbolic interactionism and is defined as the ability to induce cooperation in others (Fligstein, 2001, 2008). Skilled social actors take their actions depending on the current level of the organisation of the field, their place in that field, and the current moves by other groups in the field (2008: 230–233).

The social field concept has been widely recognised as holding the potential to confront the issue of agency and structure efficiently, and it has also informed many empirical findings (Fligstein, 2001). It has been increasingly employed in scholarly attempts concerned with a variety of social phenomena ranging from cultural studies (McNay, 1999; Schirato and Webb, 2003; Adams, 2006; Bottero, 2010; Golob and Makarovič, 2018) to studies of political (Turner, 1974; Laumann and Knoke, 1987; de Nooy, 2003; Jurak and Pinterič, 2012, Lubbers et al., 2020) and economic influences on collective action and institutional change (Hannan and Freeman, 1984; Hamilton and Biggart, 1988; Fløysand and Jakobsen, 2002; Beckert, 2010; Rončević, 2012; Rončević and Modic, 2011, Cepoi and Golob, 2017).

3. Innovations as Social Fields

To elucidate the interrelation between social structures and the role of the agents participating in the local, national, and global spheres within systems of innovations, we deploy an idea of strategic action fields. Taking into account the multidimensional form of adaptation, by which a nation, region, locality or organisation can successfully adjust to global challenges, our focus is on the meso-level of the adjustment, which provokes questions about the ability of a social setting to continuously (re)produce technological and social innovations.

The integrated theory of strategic action fields explains how stability and change are achieved by social actors in circumscribed social (Fligstein and McAdam, 2011; 2012). It consists of three main components. The first refers to the idea that the fundamental units of collective action in society are strategic action fields. They present 'a meso-level social order where actors (who can be individual or collective) interact with knowledge of one another under a set of common understandings about the purposes of the field, the relationships in the field (including who has power and why), and the field's rules' (Fligstein and McAdam, 2011: 3).

Strategic social fields can be defined as the basic structural building block of modern political/organisational life in the economy, civil society, and the state (Fligstein and McAdam, 2012: 3). The idea is linked to the work of Bourdieu and Wacquant (1992), DiMaggio and Powel (1983), Fligstein (1996), Martin (2003), and Meyer and Scott (1983), seeing that the concern with stability and change in field-level dynamics plays a central role (ibid.). The second component of the theory considers 'any given field as embedded in a broader environment consisting of countless *proximate* or *distal fields*, as well as states, which are themselves organised as [an] intricate system of strategic action fields' (Fligstein and McAdam, 2012: 3). The third component, being the core of the theory, is an account of how embedded social actors seek to fashion and maintain order in a given field (ibid.)

Each social field has its internal structural settings and defines its legitimate ways of attaching meaning to those structures and actions. Regardless of level one focuses (i.e., regional, national, sectoral, transnational), any given field is embedded 'in a broader environment consisting of countless proximate or distant fields, as well as states, which are themselves organised as [an] intricate system of strategic action fields' (Fligstein and McAdam, 2012: 3). According to Beckert (2010), internal settings are subsequently are calibrated by three social forces: institutions, networks, and cognitive frames.

4. Social Forces and Innovation

We now explain how the three social forces manifest themselves on different spatially and socially constructed levels (e.g., national, regional, sectoral), which demand clarification of conceptual and methodological units. Accordingly, we address internal structural settings of fields by drawing on Beckert's (2010) distinction of three social forces consisting of institutional rules prevalent in the field, relational topographies of networks and cognitive frames structuring the perceptions of agents. We thereby exemplify the robustness of innovation systems conceptualisations relying on our *Social-Fields-Approach* (SOFIA). Our work is also in line with the push towards multi-scalar conceptualisations of innovation systems (van Lacker et al., 2016) and helps build the relevant framework for more work on a holistic view of the innovation system as the multi-layered networks of interactions, such as the work done recently on the level of activities by Pugliese et al. (2019).

Different spatially and socially constructed levels on which innovation occurs exist. The theory of innovation systems is well established: with national innovation systems being the genotype (Modic and Rončević, 2018). However, works have also been dedicated to *transnational levels,* such as macro-regional level and global level (international or global innovation system, IIS or GIS; Binz and Truffer, 2017; Carvalho et al., 2015; Walshok et al., 2014; Fromhold-Eisebith, 2007; Borras, 2004; Niosi and Bellon, 1994). Furthermore, there are *mezzo levels* below that of national (*macro*) levels with their corresponding innovation system phenotypes: regional level (Asheim et al., 2011; Cooke et al., 1997), sectoral level (sectoral innovation systems, SIS; Faber and Hoppe; 2013; Malerba, 2002) and local level (Ferretti and Parmentola, 2015). Another perspective is that of the *micro level*, with works dedicated to technological (technological innovation system, TIS; Bergek et al., 2008; Carlsson, 1997; Carlsson and Stankiewicz, 1991) and organisational levels (van Lancker et al., 2016).

These levels of innovations can be grounded in the *spatial dimension* (i.e., macro-regional, national, regional, local) or be predominantly *a-spatial in terms of its geographic dimension* (sectorial, technology and organisational level). Whereas de la Mothe and Paquet (1998) claim there are two important elements to innovation systems (IS): *the geographical concentration* and *collective learning*, the first is defined by the notion of innovation systems as a-spatial concepts (Ter Wal and Boschma, 2011: 920). For example, the concept of 'local innovation system' can be used to identify a space where the process of collective learning and innovation activity is localised, but where, despite its name, this process is not necessarily limited to occurring within the local geographical borders (Ferretti and Parmentola, 2015). Hence, the element of collective learning is often put in the forefront, sometimes to enrich and sometimes to mitigate the problem of the spatial conceptualisation of the IS (Oinas and Malecki, 2002; Rutten and Boekema, 2007). However, there are at least two benefits of co-presence or co-location: *firstly*, this proximity serves as a powerful means to participate in the process of creating institutions (e.g., Storper and Venables, 2002; Bathelt et al., 2004). *Secondly*, actors benefit from sharing the same language and attitudes towards technology and interpretative schemes (Lawson and Lorenz, 1999; Brown and Duguid, 2000).

Not surprisingly, demarcating boundaries of what overlapping systems are is difficult, especially between those Cooke (2004) calls *proximate*, and several scholars have argued that boundaries often remain fuzzy (Markusen, 1996; Chung, 2002; Asheim, 2011; van Lancker et al., 2016), with various systems being each other's subsystems, and often not being based on pre-defined territorial boundaries, but on actor networks, governing institutions, and cognitive frameworks. In this line, Cooke (2004: 3), for example, defines regional innovation systems (RIS) as 'interacting knowledge generation and exploitation subsystems linked to global, national and other regional systems. We need to take into account that RIS as (non-state) fields are thus embedded in a complex web of other fields (Fligstein and McAdam, 2012); *vertically* with national and macro-regional innovation systems; and are simultaneously intervened or *horizontally*, with other proximate fields such as sectorial innovation systems. With the analogy of Markusen's (1996: 293) description of industrial districts, innovation systems can also be described as 'sticky places in slippery space'.

We turn now to individual social forces. The idea that institutions, social networks and cognitive frames structure innovations has already been extensively empirically verified. However, many of these studies focused independently on institutions (Hargadon and Douglas, 2001; Kenney, 2000), social networks (Powell et al., 2012; Whittington et al., 2009) or cognitive frames (Kaplan and Tripsas, 2009). Nonetheless, institutions, social networks or cognitive frames have also been repeatedly confirmed as relevant in determining the rich variety of outcomes (Fligstein and Dauter, 2007: 106–107; Beckert, 2010: 605), including those connected to innovations (Fløysand and Jakobsen, 2011; Powell et al., 2012; Rončević 2012, Rončević and Modic 2012; Modic and Rončević, 2018; Cepoi and Golob, 2017; Cepoi, 2020; Erman, 2020).

We argue that the SOFIA approach is informative on all spatially and socially constructed levels, for example, either spatial or a-spatial innovation systems (see Figure 1). Thus in the next sections, we aim to determine how the three social forces can be conceptualised inside innovation systems, whereby

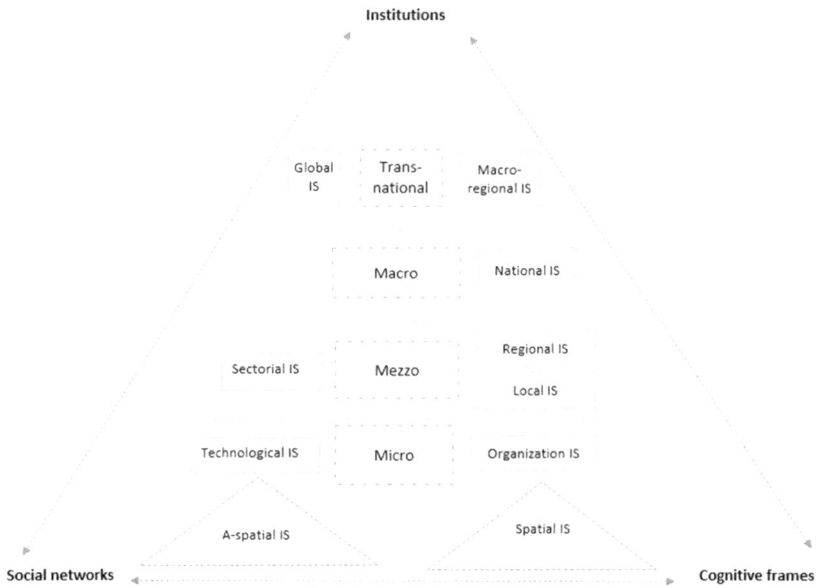

Figure 1: Social forces and innovation system

we also take into account their interaction, specifically, the mutual influence of the three social forces and the individual elements therein and focus on different levels of innovations systems, with particular emphasis on national and regional levels.

Institutions in Innovation Systems

Definitions of institutions vary, but the narrower definitions include at least rules and laws (e.g. Edquist and Johnson, 2006),[2] whereas broader definitions also include organisations (among notable examples are e.g. Nelson and Rosenberg, 1993). Through the framework political-administrative regulations (provisions, and laws), public authorities can influence the economic actors and

2 Many (especially national) innovation systems' authors rely on Norton's definition of institutions (1981) as: . . . a set of rules, compliance procedures, and moral and ethical behavioral norms designed to constrain the behavior of individuals in the interests of maximizing the wealth or utility of principals'.

their behaviour (Jakobsen and Aarset, 2010). These regulations can facilitate or hinder the innovation processes and other processes which are linked to them.

For example, based on a regional innovation systems approach, we can observe that there are (at least) two levels we need to take into account (national and regional); this is also one of the conceptual hang-ups of the regional approach, as some argue that it is not enough to focus on the subnational system level, but that regional innovation systems could only develop if rules and regulations at the level of the nation-state establish the preconditions for this to occur (e.g., Freeman, 2002). According to Cooke et al. (1997: 480), the region has governance capacities over local territories and a level of cohesion that distinguishes it from the overall state and from the other regions. In general, institutions as rules, regardless of the authority bringing them to life, limit the scope of actions by individual private or public actors by encouraging some actions and discouraging others (e.g., via innovation support legislation).

Looking at institutions in a broader sense, several types of actors need to be taken into account, both private and government (*internal* regarding the region) and *external* (mostly state) (Fligstein and McAdam, 2012). Among *internal*, special emphasis has been lately given to support services or intermediate actors, with studies on technology parks and technology transfer entities (Vasquez-Urriago et al., 2016; Guadix, 2016) and regional entities for innovation support with regional development (or innovation) agencies playing a significant role (Bellini et al., 2012). These can not only (co-)construct institutional barriers as well as create incentives but also can help understand what actions are possible and sometimes interpret the role (or the power) of individual actors. In the innovation field, they often struggle to define some (more specific) collective interest but often do quite well by steering regional consortia and acting as 'meeting' points. Other often-emphasised actors are also universities, seen as generators of local development through knowledge creation and training capabilities. Universities will add to the innovation capabilities when and if the knowledge is transferred to (local/regional) firms. Silicon Valley is a well-known case where the universities' specific relational capacities, directed at promoting and financing entrepreneurial initiatives, progressively created a relational network where the universities have been both cause and effect of strongly innovative processes (Ferretti and Parmentola, 2015).

Social Networks in Innovation Systems

Innovation systems are complex systems in which the interaction of actors is inevitable. Following this line of argument, in order to have innovation as an outcome, different stakeholders must collaborate. Therefore, the social setting forces them to act together because the exchange of resources and knowledge is necessary. The cooperation leads to the creation of long-term alliances, which is a characteristic of the innovation process (Jakobsen and Aarset, 2010, 929). Consequently, innovation happens in the presence of various collaborative arrangements, which are seen as a fundamental feature of the economic activity (Beckert, 1999). As Beckert highlights, within these arrangements, each party has its own knowledge about their internal capabilities and how these can contribute to the innovation process. Nevertheless, the role of networks does not rely only on the role of developing the innovation itself. Also, when accepted by the internal network circle, these will also have the roles of promotion, change, and diffusion of innovations (Kolleck, 2013).

When looking at social networks as a social force, we need to pay attention to university-industry cooperation as well as inter-firm collaborations, as important lubricants (Rončević and Modic, 2011; Fric and Rončević, 2018; Fric et al., 2020). Furthermore, since borders of regional innovation systems are difficult to observe, we need to account for the power of networks that extend beyond the observed system (or, alternatively, design very rigid borders). The relational networks created are the vehicles for knowledge and information exchange, thus enriching the territorial knowledge base and affecting the cognitive frames. To sum up: social networks position individuals and collectives in the social space, either limiting ties with specific nodes or encouraging them.

Todtling and Kaufmann (1999), in contrast, emphasise that the central elements are the firms that belong to the region's principal industrial sectors, flanked by those that operate in complementary sectors. Inside the innovation field, *incumbents and challengers* (Fligstein and McAdam, 2012) are well mirrored, with innovation leaders using their reputation, their links with other actors (building either innovation pools or strong consortia) as well as institutions as rules (also specifically the intellectual property rights regimes) to reinforce or keep their position of power. Firms (both incumbents and challengers) compose different types of networks that operate both within the region and beyond its boundaries, based on supplier-client relationships, cooperation and information exchange. A more comprehensive view can hence be gained by including inside the studies in this field broader network parameters or include variables that will envelop extra-regional networks (e.g. extra-regional innovation cooperation) that influence the innovative process (Coe and Bunnel, 2001).

Cognitive Frames in Innovation Systems

If institutions and networks seem straightforward explanations of economic results, in contrast, cognition in modern literature plays a less significant role in explaining economic results (Fligstein, 2001). Nevertheless, cognitive frames are linked to perceptions (Beckert, 2010). Additionally, we turn our focus to the aspect of adaptability, which is primordial for modern based economies. At the same time, market flexibility is important, as is their response toward new challenges (Wachsen and Blind, 2016). Therefore, having a greater level of openness toward the ideas that come from the outside contribute to the development of R&D performance (Drechsler and Natter, 2012) and innovation.

Cognitive frames can also be studied in more detail in RIS; since, on the national level, the unit of observation is the whole country, as if there would be no 'mountains in a flat world'. Nevertheless, we know there are outliers in many countries, from the North-European leaders such as Stockholm, to Argonauts in Shenzhen. The latter are trying to mimic the very successful example of Silicon Valley and its neighbouring Hong Kong by establishing a similar innovation milieu. For innovation in high-performing regions (or spaces), authors often note very specific cognitive frames. Thus, some authors argue that even the regional level is too broad and that innovation systems are often localised in even more restricted areas (Rantisi, 2002).

Cognitive frames act as mental tool-kits; the emphasis therein is given to several elements, such as the centrality of firms; the trust inside the system; the presence of a skilled workforce and companies' commitment to R&D. Cognitive frames enable interpreting relevant strategies, such as the introduction and nurturing of firm-based innovation and the ability to absorb new knowledge and its translation into innovations (products). These scripts also suggest social action for all the involved actors that have their basis in institutions as rules, as well as previous and potential relationships with other actors. They help individual actors interact by providing a common understanding about the purpose in the certain field, the (power) relationships and the field's rules (institutions in a narrower sense). It seems the concept of cognitive frames can conceptually be more easily accepted on lower, and especially a-spatial, levels of innovation system conceptualisations; for example, its close ties to organisational theory make authors within organisation innovation systems more perceptive.

5. Purpose of This Volume: Showcasing the Applicability of SOFIA

This chapter and the subsequent volume revolve around the *Social-Fields-Approach* (SOFIA) as an approach to conceptualisation and operationalisation for the purpose of empirical research. Part of this volume uses the SOFIA approach as such; others elaborate or empirically validate different elements related to it – as a whole, the volume contributes to the further honing of SOFIA. The used acronym 'SOFIA' has not been coined by accident, as it corresponds to the Greek word 'Σοφία', meaning wisdom

In the present chapter, we approach innovation processes in the context of the three social forces, opening the possibility of understanding these processes from a broader perspective in various milieus, i.e. spatial spheres. This introductory chapter thus frames the SOFIA approach and acts as a signal post for the rest of the volume.

Other chapters in this volume further the application of SOFIA, or its individual aspects, on the exploration of innovation in the context of the European Union and its grand strategies. The first section is composed of two chapters that shed some light on European-level policymaking. Petra Kleindienst discusses the issue of artificial intelligence in the context of fundamental values, and Cristian Gangaliuc touches upon regional innovation policy.

The second section of this volume deals with Innovation 2.0 in a regional context. Tamara Besednjak Valič engages the social fields perspective in her take on open innovation and its impact on inter-organisational stability and sustainable growth. Urška Fric also deals with sustainable growth but with a focus on open innovation as a path-maker for the circular economy.

In the final section, Alenka Pandiloska Jurak explores the implementation of SOFIA in the context of technologies, innovation and regional policy, and Victor Cepoi demonstrates the application of SOFIA in the context of a small-n qualitative comparative case study of Ireland and Slovenia.

This volume contributes a new perspective and approach in research on innovation. We believe that SOFIA can have implications for both academic research and practical applications in reshaping the existing instruments and governance arrangements in innovation policy. Whilst applying SOFIA, we urge researchers to leverage the plurality of different qualitative, quantitative and mixed-method approaches in innovation studies, including less conventional methods, such as QCA (Ragin, 2008). Diligent application of SOFIA can also subsequently lead to the development of high-level theoretical contributions.

Notably, the approach can be used beyond the innovation research, which is, to some extent, visible from various chapters in this volume. Thus, we not only encourage further adoptions of SOFIA in fields beyond the innovation field, but we also encourage further elaboration of related concepts. Various approaches and their research 'templates' can be helpful in the sense of providing standards and increasing rigour and comparability of research. Nonetheless, not all issues and explored phenomena fit existing dominant 'templates'. SOFIA provides an alternative to existing approaches and thus enriches the available 'toolbox' of approaches.

References

Adams, M. (2006) Hybridizing habitus and reflexivity: towards an understanding of contemporary identity? *Sociology*, 40(3): 511–528.

Balzat, M. and Hanusch, H. (2004) Recent trends in the research on national innovation systems. *Journal of Evolutionary Economics*, 14(2): 197–210.

Beckert, J. (2010) How do fields change? The interrelations of institutions, networks, and cognition in the dynamics of markets. *Organization Studies*, 31(5): 605–627.

Bellini, N., Danson, M. and Halkier, H. (eds.) (2012) *Regional Development Agencies: The Next Generation?: Networking, Knowledge and Regional Policies.* London and New York: Routledge.

Binz, C. and Truffer, B. (2017) Global Innovation Systems – A conceptual framework for innovation dynamics in transnational contexts. *Research Policy*, 46(7): 1284–1298.

Borrás, S. (2004) System of innovation theory and the European Union. *Science and Public Policy*, 31(6): 425–433.

Bottero, W. (2010) Intersubjectivity and Bourdieusian approaches to 'identity'. *Cultural Sociology*, 4 (1): 3–22.

Bourdieu, P. (1977) *Outline of a Theory of Practice*. Cambridge: Cambridge University Press.

Bourdieu, P. (1990) *The Logic of Practice*. Stanford, CA: Stanford University Press.

Bourdieu, P. and Wacquant, L. (1992) *An Invitation to Reflexive Sociology.* Cambridge: Polity Press.

Brown, J.S. and Duguid, P. (2000) Balancing act: How to capture knowledge without killing it. *Harvard Business Review*, 78(May-June): 73–80.

Carlsson, B. and Stankiewicz, R. (1991) On the nature, function and composition of technological systems. *Journal of Evolutionary Economics*, 1(2): 93–118.

Carvalho, N., Carvalho, L. and Nunes, S. (2015) A methodology to measure innovation in European Union through the national innovation system. *International Journal of Innovation and Regional Development*, 6(2): 159–180.

Cepoi, V. (2019) Interplay of social forces: A focus on regional innovation processes. *The Social Sciences*, 14(12): 423–430.

Cepoi, V. (2020) A meta-analysis and explanation of innovation processes through the outline of social fields theory. *Research in Social Change*, 12(3): 15–31. DOI: 10.2478/rsc-2020-0012.

Cepoi, V. and Golob, T. (2017) Innovation performance in the EU comparative perspective: The interplay of social forces in the context of national innovation systems. *Comparative Sociology*, 16(4): 555–579.

Chung, S. (2002) Building a national innovation system through regional innovation systems. *Technovation*, 22(8): 485–491.

Coe, N.M. and Bunnell, T.G. (2001) Spaces and scales of innovation. *Progress in Human Geography*, 25(4): 569–589.

Cooke, P. (1992) Regional innovation systems: Competitive regulation in the new Europe. *Geoforum*, 23(3): 365–382.

Cooke, P. (2004) Introduction: Regional innovation systems – an evolutionary approach. In: Cooke, P., Heindreich, M. and Braczyk, H.J. (eds.) *Regional Innovation Systems: The Role of Governance in a Globalised World*. 2nd Edition. London: Routledge, pp. 1–18.

Cooke, P., Uranga, M.G. and Etxebarria G. (1997) Regional innovation systems: Institutional and organizational dimensions. *Research Policy*, 26(4–5): 475–491.

de la Mothe, J. and Paquet, G. (eds.) (1998) *Local and Regional Systems of Innovation*. Dordrecht: Kluwer.

De Nooy, W. (2003) Fields and networks: Correspondence analysis and social network analysis in the framework of field theory. *Poetics*, 31(5–6): 305–27.

DiMaggio, P. and Powel, W. (1983) The iron cage revisited: Institutional isomorphism and collective rationality in organizational fields. *American Sociological Review* 48(2): 147–160.

Džajić Uršič, E. (2020) *Morphogenesis of Industrial Symbiotic Networks*. Berlin: Peter Lang.

Erman, N. (2020) Prospects for innovation performance on European level. *Research in Social Change*, 12(3): 100–114. DOI: 10.2478/rsc-2020-0016.

Ferretti, M. and Parmentola, A. (2015) *The Creation of Local Innovation Systems in Emerging Countries*. Heidelberg, New York, Dordrecht, London: Springer Briefs in Regional Science.

Fligstein, N. (2001) Social skill and the theory of fields. *Sociological Theory*, 19(2): 105–125.

Fligstein, N. (2008) *Euroclash: The EU, European Identity and the Future of Europe*. Oxford: Oxford University Press.

Fligstein, N. and Dauter, L. (2007) The sociology of markets. *Annual Review of Sociology*, 33: 105–128.

Fligstein, N. and McAdam, D. (2011) Toward a general theory of strategic action fields. *Sociological Theory*, 29(1): 1–26.

Fligstein, N. and McAdam, D. (2012) *A Theory of Fields*. Oxford: Oxford University Press.

Fløysand, A. and Jakobsen, S.-E. (2002) Clusters, social fields and capabilities: Rules and restructuring in Norwegian fish processing clusters. *International Studies of Management and Organisation*, 31(4): 35–55.

Fløysand, A., & Jakobsen, S. E. (2011). The complexity of innovation: A relational turn. *Progress in Human Geography*, 35(3), 328–344.

Freeman, C. (2002) Continental, national and sub-national innovation systems – complementarity and economic growth. *Research Policy*, 31(2): 191–211.

Fric, U. and Roncevic, B. (2018) E-simbioza: Leading a way to a Circular Economy through Industrial Symbiosis in Slovenia. *Socijalna ekologija*, 27(2): 119–140.

Fric, U., Rončević, B. and Džajić Uršič, E. (2020) Role of computer software tools in industrial symbiotic networks and the examination of sociocultural factors. *Environmental Progress & Sustainable Energy*, 39(2): e13364.

Fromhold-Eisebith, M. (2007) Bridging scales in innovation policies: How to link regional, national and international innovation systems. *European Planning Studies*, 15(2): 217–233.

Golob, T. and Makarovič, M. (2018) Student mobility and transnational social ties as factors of reflexivity. *Social Sciences*, 7: 46.

Guadix, J., Carrillo-Castrillo, J., Onieva, L. and Navascues, J. (2016) Success variables in science and technology parks. *Journal of Business Research*, 69(11): 4870–4875.

Hamilton, G. and Biggart, N. (1988) Market, culture and authority. *American Journal of Sociology*, 94(supplement): s52–s94.

Hannan, M. and Freeman, J. (1984) Structural inertia and organizational change. *American Sociological Review*, 49(2): 149–164.

Hargadon, A. B. and Douglas, Y. (2001) When innovations meet institutions: Edison and the design of the electric light. *Administrative Science Quarterly* 46(3): 476–501.

Hesse, Mary B. (1970). *Forces and Fields: The Concept of Action at a Distance in the History of Physics*. Westport, CT: Greenwood.

Kaplan, S. and Tripsas, M. (2008) Thinking about technology: Applying a cognitive lens to technical change. *Research Policy*, 37(5): 790–805.

Kenney, M. (2000) *Understanding Silicon Valley: The Anatomy of an Entrepreneurial Region*. Stanford: Stanford University Press.

Laumann, E. and Knoke, D. (1987) *The Organizational State*. Madison, WI: University of Wisconsin Press.

Lawson, C. and Lorenz, E. (1999) Collective learning, tacit knowledge and regional innovative capacity. *Regional Studies,* 33(4): 305–17.

Lewin, K. (1951) *Field Theory in Social Science*. New York: Harper.

Lubbers, M. J., Verdery, A. M. and Molina, J. L. (2020) Social networks and transnational social fields: A review of quantitative and mixed-methods approaches. *International Migration Review,* 54(1): 177–204.

Martin, L. J. (2003) What is field theory? *American Journal of Sociology,* 109(1): 1–49.

Martin, L. J. and Gregg, F. (2015) Was Bourdieu a field theorist? In: Hilgers, M. and Mangez, E. (eds.) *Bourdieu's Theory of Social Fields*. London and New York: Routledge, Taylor & Francis, pp. 39–61.

Maskell, P., Bathelt, H. and Malmberg, A. (2006) Building global knowledge pipelines: The role of temporary clusters. *European Planning Studies*, 14(8): 997–1013.

McNay, L. (1999) Gender, habitus and the field: Pierre Bourdieu and the limits of reflexivity. *Theory, Culture and Society* 16(1): 95–117.

Meyer, J. W. and Scott, W. R. (1983) *Organizational Environments: Ritual and Rationality.* London: Sage.

Modic, D., Roncevic, B. (2018). Social topography for sustainable innovation policy: Putting institutions, social networks and cognitive frames in their place. *Comparative Sociology,* 17(1): 100–127.

Niosi, J. and Bellon, B. (1994) The global interdependence of national innovation systems: Evidence, limits, and implications. *Technology in Society*, 16(2): 173–197.

Oinas, P. and Malecki, E.J. (2002) The evolution of technologies in time and space: From national and regional to spatial innovation systems. *International Regional Science Review*, 25(1): 102–131.

Pandiloska Jurak, A. and Pinterič, U. (2012) Assessment of municipalities'performances in Slovenia. *Transylvanian Review of Administrative Sciences,* 35: 121–137.

Powell, W. W., Packalen, K. and Whittington, K. (2012) Organizational and institutional genesis: The Emergence of High-Tech Clusters in the Life Sciences. In: Padget, J.F. and Powel, W. (eds.) *The Emergence of Organizations and Markets*. Princeton: Princeton University Press, pp. 434–465.

Pugliese, E., Cimini, G., Patelli, A., Zaccaria, A., Pietronero, L., and Gabrielli, A. (2019) Unfolding the innovation system for the development of countries: Coevolution of Science, Technology and Production. *Scientific reports*, 9(1): 1–12.

Ragin, C. (2008) *Redesigning Social Inquiry: Fuzzy Sets and Beyond*. Chicago: University of Chicago Press.

Rantisi, N.M. (2002) The local innovation system as a source of 'variety': Openness and adaptability in New York City's garment district. *Regional Studies* 36(6): 587–602.

Roncevic, B. (2012). Regional development agencies and changing social fields: Towards a sociology of regional systems of innovation. In: Bellini, N., Danson, M. and Halkier, H. (eds.) *Regional Development Agencies: The Next Generation?: Networking, Knowledge and Regional Policies, (Regions and cities, 59)*. London; New York: Routledge, pp. 87–101.

Roncevic, B. and Dolores, M. (2011) Regional systems of innovations as social fields. *Sociologija i prostor: časopis za istraživanje prostornoga i sociokulturnog razvoja*. 49(191): 313–333.

Rončević, B. and Modic, D. (2012) Social fields of technological innovations. In: Genov, N. (ed.) *Global Trends and Regional Development*. New York: Routledge, pp. 226–247.

Rončević, B., Makarovič, M., Tomšič, M. and Cepoi, V. (2018) Methodological solutions for comparative research on transformations. In: Vihalemm, P., Masso, A., and Opermann, S. (eds.) *The Routledge International Handbook of European Social Transformations*. Abingdon and New York: Routledge, pp. 57–70.

Rutten, R. and Boekema, F. (2007) Spatial innovation systems: Theory and cases – an introduction. *European Planning Studies*, 15(2): 171–177.

Schirato, T. and Webb, J. (2003) *Understanding Globalization*. London and New Delhi: Sage.

Storper, M. and Venables, A.J. (2004) Buzz: Face-to-face contact and the urban economy. *Journal of Economic Geography*, 4(4): 351–370.

Ter Wal, A. and Boschma, R. (2011) Co-evolution of firms, industries and networks in space. *Regional Studies*, 45(7): 919–933.

Turner, V.W. (1974) *Dramas, Fields and Metaphors: Symbolic Action in Human Society*. Ithaca, NY: Cornell University Press.

Vasquez-Urriago, A.R., Barge-Gil, A. and Modrego R.A. (2016) Science and technology parks and cooperation for innovation: Empirical evidence from Spain. *Research Policy*, 45(1): 137–147.

Walshok, M. L., Shapiro, J. D. and Owens, N. (2014) Transnational innovation networks aren't all created equal: Towards a classification system. *The Journal of Technology Transfer*, 39(3): 345–357.

Weber, M. (1946) *Essays in Sociology;* translated, edited, and with an introduction by H. H. Gerth and C. Wright Mills. New York: Oxford University Press.

Whittington, K. B., Owen-Smith, J. and Powell, W. W. (2009) Networks, propinquity, and innovation in knowledge-intensive industries. *Administrative Science Quarterly*, 54(1): 90–122.

Wilkinson, K. P. (1970) Community as a social field. *Social Forces,* 48(3): 311–322

EU, Grand Strategies, and Policy-Making

Petra Kleindienst

The EU Strategies and Policies on Artificial Intelligence and Their Impact on Fundamental Values

Abstract: Artificial intelligence represents one of the most pertinent threats to human dignity. The emergence of artificial intelligence-based technology raises the question of how to protect human dignity in the face of quickly changing technologies. In this regard, EU strategies and policies on artificial intelligence must address the safeguarding of human dignity. Moreover, it is essential that EU strategies and policies on artificial intelligence consider human dignity in a comprehensive manner, understanding a two-dimensional concept consisting of initial and realised dignity. This chapter reveals some inconsistencies in some EU strategies and policies on artificial intelligence when defining and interpreting human dignity. Additionally, the chapter shows that some EU policies and strategies on artificial intelligence sometimes refer to human dignity merely superficially. In this regard, the chapter represents 'Ethics Guidelines for Trustworthy Artificial Intelligence' as a relatively good example of an EU document when with regard to the concept of human dignity. As the relationship between institutional systems and cultural platforms of society is mutually reinforcing, it is crucial that EU policies and strategies reflect the relevance of human dignity.

Keywords: European Union, strategies, policies, artificial intelligence, human dignity

1. Introduction

In April 2018, the European strategy for artificial intelligence (AI) was presented, which is not surprising, since AI is one of the key emerging issues of the information society (Rončević and Tomšič, 2017). According to this document, the European Union (EU) should have a coordinated approach to make the most of the opportunities offered by AI and to address the new challenges that it brings (European Commission, 2018a). In February 2020, the European Commission released the White Paper 'On Artificial Intelligence – A European approach to excellence and trust' (European Commission, 2020a). The white paper sets out policy options on achieving a regulatory and investment-oriented approach with the twin objectives of promoting the uptake of AI and addressing the risks associated with certain uses of this new technology. The EU has a tradition of ambitious grand strategies (Makarovič et al., 2014) and, as a part of this, it is striving to become a global leader in innovation in the data economy and its applications as set out in the European data strategy, combining European technological and industrial strengths with high-quality digital infrastructure and a regulatory framework based on its fundamental values (European Commission, 2020a, 2020b).

AI systems can have large individual as well as societal impacts. From the societal perspective, the use of AI systems can have a significant role in achieving the Sustainable Development Goals and supporting the democratic process and social rights; it can also influence the attainment of the goals of the European Green Deal.[6] Europe is leading the way in tackling climate and environmental-related challenges. Digital technologies such as AI are critical enablers for attaining the goals of the Green Deal (European Commission, 2019a; European Commission, 2020b).

From the perspective of an individual, it is vital that AI is grounded on the EU's values and fundamental rights as the use of AI can affect the values on which the EU is founded and lead to breaches of fundamental rights (European Commission, 2020a; Council of Europe, 2018). Values are highly relevant for the functioning of political systems and society; they are crucial elements in the process of collective identification (Golob, 2014; Golob, Kristovič in Makarovič, 2014; Makarovič in Golob, 2015), which especially applies to the concept of human dignity. AI must be grounded on human dignity since we can regard it as 'the foundation and justification for rights and duties: because of human dignity, human beings have rights and duties' (Shultziner, 2003). Today, it would be hard to imagine an international document on human rights that is not based on human dignity (Kleindienst, 2017). In the EU context, human dignity is regarded as a general principle to be followed by all Member States (ibid.).

According to SOFIA, which implies the importance of three social forces (institutions, social networks and cognitive frames), institutions make certain cultural meanings socially relevant (Beckert, 2010). In this way, the institutions can influence the cognitive frames which shape the structure of social networks. However, this approach, which has been developing for the past decade primarily to study the social underpinnings of innovations (Rončević, 2012, 2020; Roncevic and Modic, 2011, 2012, 2018; Rončević et al., 2018; Rončević and Besednjak, 2019), was designed to be applied in a variety of social fields. Considering the meaning of human dignity in the context of the EU's values and fundamental rights, it is relevant to answer the research question about how EU strategies and policies on AI rely on the human dignity concept; and how they define and interpret it.

Today, we stand on the cusp of a new age of AI in which the very concept of who and what is counted as human may once again be up for debate (Kanuck, 2019). The EU needs to consider all the changes that could be brought by adopting strategies and policies on AI, especially in the context of main values upon which the EU is based. It is particularly relevant to be aware of how the adoption of existing EU strategies and policies on AI influences the relevance of the human dignity concept as the leading EU principle.

2. Human Dignity

To achieve the aim of this chapter, it is relevant to understand what the concept of human dignity is. According to Kleindienst and Tomšič (2017), the understanding and normative operationalisation of human dignity have strong repercussions in both legal and political terms. However, despite the broad theoretical dimensions of human dignity and frequent references to it in numerous legal acts and other documents, this concept is characterised by the absence of its clear, unequivocal and coherent, universally valid definition. The latter is not provided either by international legal documents or by documents of the Council of Europe and the European Union, or as national legal acts.

The phenomenon of human dignity is to be understood as a multifaceted concept intertwined with several disciplines (law, political science, bioethics, medicine, etc.) and characterised by the extensive legal, moral and political philosophy of many authors in which human dignity was framed and given meaning (see Donnelly, 2013; Dupré, 2015; Kateb, 2011; Rosen, 2012; McCrudden et al., 2013; Waldron, 2013; Barak, 2015; Kleindienst, 2017, 2019; Gilabert, 2018; Golob, 2020; Mahmoudi and Penn, 2020). Sensen (2011) identifies two paradigms of human dignity, a traditional and contemporary one. The traditional paradigm has dominated throughout history, relating to some crucial authors such as Cicero (1913), Thomas Aquinas (1947), Pico della Mirandola (1496) and Immanuel Kant (1785). Sensen analysed the philosophy of these thinkers and found certain similarities between them. In regard to Sensen (2011), according to the traditional paradigm, human beings differ from the rest of nature and the other creatures in possession of certain abilities (reason, freedom, autonomy) that are either given to the human being by nature or from God. On the basis of these abilities, human beings are endowed with a special, elevated position in the universe, and thus also with human dignity (Kleindienst, 2019).

Contrary to the traditional paradigm, as Kleindienst (2019) explains, the contemporary paradigm of human dignity did not exist prior to the 20th century and is present today in the documents of the United Nations and a number of contemporary legal sources. This paradigm does not offer connections between human dignity and the possession of certain abilities (reason, freedom, autonomy) and therefore differs significantly from the traditional paradigm, which can be recognised in the philosophy of some of the above-mentioned thinkers.

According to Sensen (2011), a contemporary paradigm denotes human dignity as a 'non-relational property' (i.e., a characteristic that exists independently from anything else; an objective and inherent human characteristic that cannot be changed under any circumstances in which people find themselves). Human beings, having this characteristic, hold a special immanent and objective value, which allows them to claim rights against other people subsequently. As explained by Sensen, in the contemporary paradigm, we follow Seifert's ontologically oriented theory, based on intuitionism (Moore, 1903).[1] However, not all advocates of the contemporary paradigm follow intuitionism, with some presenting different arguments for the absolute value of human beings, particularly in relation to rational human nature (see Korsgaard, 1996; Wood, 1999). (Kleindienst, 2019).

By distinguishing between the traditional and the contemporary paradigm of human dignity, Sensen implies that we cannot rely on history when referring to the contemporary paradigm, since those are two different patterns of thinking. A new pattern of thinking is also indicated by some researchers' views that the inherent human dignity of a person cannot depend on the possession of certain abilities of that person, but should be based solely on the fact that the person belongs to the human species (see, for example, Sulmasy, 2008; Gastmans and De Lepeleire, 2010; Kleindienst, 2018). Additionally, by relating human dignity to the capability of reason or human autonomy (i.e., traditional paradigm), it is not possible to explain all existing cases. For example, with the traditional paradigm, it can no longer be explained that people in vegetative state are endowed with human dignity, as they cannot use their reasoning abilities in real life situations, as well as they cannot rely on their autonomy when following self-fulfilment. Thus, a follow-up to Sensen's theory is inevitably necessary (Kleindienst, 2018).

1 Moore (1903), as a typical author of intuitionism, presented natural characteristics (those that are essential for the creation of a human being and can be tested) and unnatural characteristics. Other relevant typical authors of intuitionism include W. D. Ross, A. C. Ewing, H. A. Prichard, H. J. McCloskey.

Furthermore, scientific findings (Formosa in Mackenzie, 2014; Sensen, 2011; Kleindienst, 2017, 2019) show that the contemporary concept of human dignity should be regarded as a concept comprising two basic dimensions: (1) initial dignity and (2) realised dignity. According to Kleindienst and Tomšič (2017; see also Kleindienst, 2017; Kleindienst, 2019) initial dignity, the first dimension of human dignity, implies a respectable status of a person or the status of absolute human intrinsic value. It indicates the dimension of human dignity that belongs to a human being due to the mere fact that he/she is placed into a group of human beings. It stems from human nature as such and distinguishes human beings from members of other species. It thus constitutes a kind of metaphysical element, which is inseparably linked to humans and, as such, existing in any space and time (and therefore universal). Considering the fact that all human beings are endowed with the initial dignity, as human beings, we could conclude that it is exactly the initial dignity, which constitutes the essence of man. We could also say that initial dignity constitutes a human being, which is why it is referred to as a 'constitutive element' of man or of personal identity. Inseparability between this element and members of the human species is what makes human beings exceptional and gives them a special value. It is a permanent, stable dignity, which does not have different stages. It simply exists within human beings, while its scope is not measurable; it belongs to every man to exactly the same extent: to the extent that makes humans exceptional and excellent. To be a human being therefore means to be a carrier of initial dignity, which implies that it is his/her inalienable humanity that brings respect to an individual (ibid.).

Realised dignity is a dimension of human dignity that tells us the extent to which human dignity is realised/implemented in the case of a particular individual, which means that while every human being is born with initial dignity, they do not necessarily simultaneously enjoy realised dignity. In contrast to initial dignity, realised dignity is, in fact, precarious and unstable (it may only be temporary). It can have different levels; thus, someone can have a higher or lower level of realised dignity than their fellow human. When we say someone has lost their dignity, we are talking of realised dignity. Similarly, 'dignified behaviour' also refers to realised dignity and characterises behaviour corresponding to a subject endowed with initial dignity (Kleindienst, 2017; Kleindienst and Tomšič, 2017; Kleindienst, 2019).

The degree of realised dignity in accordance with our concept consists of two elements that are both necessary to fully encapsulate realised dignity: (1) man's relation to oneself (self-respect); and (2) man's relation to their fellow man (and vice versa) (Kleindienst, 2017; Kleindienst and Tomšič, 2017; Kleindienst, 2019).

3. EU Strategies and Policies on Artificial Intelligence and Human Dignity Concept

Broadly speaking, the term 'AI' refers to a simulation of human intelligence processes by machines such as in computer system (Ahmet, 2018). It is a science of making intelligent machines that perform tasks as well as or better than humans can (Harris, 2011). Although the term dates back to the 1950s, AI originated as a research area before the term 'AI' was coined (Flasiński, 2017). It generally involves borrowing characteristics from human intelligence and applying them as algorithms in a computer-friendly way (Arelli, 2018). The European Commission (2018a) defines AI as 'systems that display intelligent behaviour by analysing their environment and taking actions – with some degree of autonomy – to achieve specific goals'. Therefore, AI is no longer science fiction and is shaping our daily practices as well as a fast-growing number of fundamental aspects of our societies (Cath et al., 2018). It is accelerating rapidly and it will certainly immensely affect the future of the human race. Given the major impact that AI can have on our society and the need to build trust, it is vital that European AI is grounded in our values and fundamental rights (European Commission, 2020a; Council of Europe, 2018). In this context, relying on the human dignity concept is crucial when adopting EU strategies and policies on AI.

In general, the emergence of AI can have positive as well as negative impacts on the human dignity of an individual. Zardiashvili and Fosch-Villaronga (2020), for example, illustrate positive and negative impacts of AI on human dignity in the healthcare domain. They show that AI in healthcare, namely healthcare applications of robots,[2] might support individuals in achieving dignity and at the same time, pressure it. On the one hand, the usage of such robots could elevate one's self-confidence, autonomy, and feeling of independence

2 Zardiashvili and Fosch-Villaronga (2020) list the most relevant robot applications in healthcare domain:
- *Feeding robots*: the incorporation of robotic arms in tables, or in robotic wheelchairs with a feeding function.
- *Robots for the blind*: robots that can guide blind people.
- *Exoskeletons:* robotic devices that help users to stand up and walk again, which is a primary human function. They are also useful in rehabilitation process.
- *Sex robots*: robots that enable the disabled to experience their sexuality. The effects of sex robots are still under-researched.
- *Therapeutic robots:* robots that can act as a therapist for paranoid patients.

from the caregivers as well as enhance options of the disabled to participate in social life. Thus, such robots could encourage the disabled to gain more self-respect and positively impact their level of human dignity (see, for example, Leroux and Labruto, 2012).

On the other hand, according to the European Commission (2018b), European institutions acknowledge that human contact is an essential aspect of personal care and that the inclusion of robots could dehumanise caring practices. Such instances of human-robot interactions raise the question of to what extent the use and development of robots for healthcare applications can challenge human dignity (see Vallor, 2011; Sharkey, 2014; Fosch-Villaronga, 2019). Sometimes robot applications might be presented as the solution to bridge the loneliness that elderly or disabled persons often experience; at other times, relevant literature suggests that robot applications elevate feelings of loneliness, impair autonomy, and adjust a person's sense of self, that may challenge the concept of human dignity and result in its violation (see, e.g., Zardiashvili and Fosch-Villaronga, 2020). Recent literature also highlights that technology might have unintended long-term harmful impacts on the human psyche, particularly on the way the brain works and the person's identity, and this also raises questions of whether these technologies are adequate for care purposes (ibid.).

3.1. References to Human Dignity in EU Documents

The acceptance of the Universal Declaration of Human Rights established 'the idea that human dignity and human rights are the core values which should be respected when pursuing any policy'. Additionally, 'it establishes that human dignity and rights are afforded to all human beings' and 'that all human action must act in accordance with human dignity' (Capps, 2009; see Kleindienst, 2017). According to Kleindienst (2017), in the European Union context, human dignity represents the fundamental core. However, in the primary law of the European Union, human dignity is explicitly mentioned (in writing) only after the Lisbon Treaty (2007) was adopted. The Treaty on European Union provides that the European Union is founded on the values of respect for human dignity which, together with certain other values, is 'common to the Member States in a society in which pluralism, non-discrimination, tolerance, justice, solidarity and equality between women and men prevail' (Article 2). Human dignity is also referred to in the preamble of the EU Charter of Fundamental Rights (hereinafter referred as Charter); moreover, its first article is entitled 'Human dignity': 'Human dignity is inviolable. It must be respected and protected'.

Human dignity is mentioned in secondary European Union law and the case law of the European Court of Justice (ECJ) as well (ibid.).

This chapter focuses on AI in the light of EU strategies and policies in relation to the human dignity concept. In April 2018, European countries signed a Declaration of Cooperation on Artificial Intelligence (AI) which defines the agreement of participating member states on ensuring that human beings remain at the centre of development, deployment and decision-making of AI as well as on ensuring an adequate legal and ethical framework, building on EU fundamental rights and values. The European strategy for artificial intelligence (European Commission, 2018a) encourages the idea of placing the power of AI at the service of human progress. The EU has the main ingredients to build on in order to become a leader in the AI revolution: a strong scientific and industrial base, leading research labs and universities, recognised leadership in robotics as well as innovative start-ups. It also has a comprehensive legal framework that protects consumers while promoting innovation. Therefore, the European strategy for artificial intelligence (ibid.) sets out a European initiative on AI, which aims to: (1) Boost the EU's technological and industrial capacity and AI uptake across the economy, both by the private and public sectors; (2) prepare for socio-economic changes brought about by AI by encouraging the modernisation of education and training systems, nurturing talent, anticipating changes in the labour market, supporting labour market transitions and adaptation of social protection systems; (3) ensure an appropriate ethical and legal framework, based on the Union's values and in line with the Charter (ibid.).

The European Commission puts forward a European approach to Artificial Intelligence and Robotics. In its Communication, the European Commission (2018a), meanwhile explains one of the three main pillars that the European approach to AI is based on ('*Ensure an appropriate ethical and legal framework*'), underlining the relevance of potential impacts of AI on human dignity. Following from that, the draft of the AI Ethics Guidelines was presented by the European Commission's High-Level Expert Group on Artificial Intelligence (AI HLEG), which was followed by Ethics Guidelines for Trustworthy AI (AI HLEG, 2019). The latter conceptualised 'the respect for human dignity' as one of the fundamental rights of human being as a basis for Trustworthy AI. According to AI HLEG (2019), this right involves recognition of the inherent value of humans (i.e. a human being does not need to look a certain way, have a certain job, or live in a certain country to be valuable, we are all valuable by virtue of being human). More specifically, AI HLEG (2019) states:

> Human dignity encompasses the idea that every human being possesses an 'intrinsic worth', which can never be diminished, compromised or repressed by others – nor by new technologies like AI systems. [...] 'In the context of AI, respect for human dignity entails that all people are treated with respect due to them as individuals, rather than merely as data subjects. To specify the development or application of AI in line with human dignity, one can further articulate that AI systems are developed in a manner which serves and protects humans' physical and moral integrity, personal and cultural sense of identity as well as the satisfaction of their essential needs. (AI HLEG, 2019, 10)

From the citation above, we can conclude that AI HLEG recognises initial as well as realised dignity. By mentioning human dignity as a fundamental right that involves recognising the inherent value of humans and that encompasses the idea that every human being possesses an intrinsic worth that cannot be affected by others, AI HLEG recognises the dimension of 'initial dignity'. Thereby, EU institutions follow the 'human-centric approach' in which 'the human being enjoys a unique and inalienable moral status of primacy in the civil, political, economic and social fields' (AI HLEG, 2019, 10). Additionally, AI HLEG (2019) brings human dignity as an example of a fundamental right or correlated principle that is 'absolute and cannot be subject to a balancing exercise'.

Furthermore, by mentioning the 'respect for human dignity', which implies that all people are treated with the respect due to them as individuals, rather than merely as data subjects, AI HLEG recognises the dimension of 'realised dignity'. AI HLEG implies that rights described in the EU Charter are rooted in respect for human dignity:

> The EU Treaties and the EU Charter prescribe a series of fundamental rights that EU member states and EU institutions are legally obliged to respect when implementing EU law. These rights are described in the EU Charter by reference to dignity, freedoms, equality and solidarity, citizens' rights and justice. The common foundation that unites these rights can be understood as rooted in respect for human dignity (AI HLEG, 2019, 10).

Similarly, AI HLEG (2019) implies that fundamental rights set out in the EU Treaties 'are united by reference to a common foundation rooted in respect for human dignity' (AI HLEG, 2019, 37). AI HLEG (2019) undoubtedly shows that due to the intrinsic worth of human beings (i.e. initial dignity), people must be treated with respect, which implies the need for respect for human dignity (i.e., realised dignity). AI HLEG's implications that the intrinsic worth of human beings can never be diminished, compromised, or repressed by others are in line with the descriptions of initial dignity by Kleindienst (2017), who explains that initial dignity is completely independent of the existence of realised dignity or from the extent to which dignity was realised in the real-life case of a particular individual. Initial dignity can exist in complete isolation of a human being from the rest of the world. Even if realised dignity is completely minimised, a human being is still entitled to the initial dignity as the core of every human being. For example, deprivation and oppression of an individual by society may lead to a lower level of realised dignity; however, the initial dignity still exists in all its perfection.

In contrast, it is impossible to defend the existence of realised dignity independent of initial dignity. Realised dignity is based on initial dignity, as its 'spine' or the foundation of its function. Without initial dignity, realised dignity would lack a fundamental building block. Initial dignity can be described as a meta-assumption that enables a human being the possibility of self-realisation and respect from other people (ibid.).

3.2. Defining Human Dignity in EU Documents

However, when AI HLEG (2019) refers to human dignity as a fundamental right, it interchangeably mentions human dignity as an intrinsic worth or inherent value of human beings (i.e., initial dignity) and respect for human dignity (i.e., realised dignity). Additionally, in 2019, the Commission launched the Communication on Building Trust in Human-Centric Artificial Intelligence which denoted respect for human dignity as one of the main values on which the EU is founded. Furthermore, the 'White Paper 'On Artificial Intelligence – A European approach to excellence and trust' presents policy options to enable a trustworthy and secure development of AI in Europe, in full respect of the values and rights of EU citizens. The main building blocks of this document are: (1) the policy framework setting out measures to align efforts at European, national, and regional levels; (2) the key elements of a future regulatory framework for AI in Europe that will create a unique 'ecosystem of trust' (European Commission, 2020a). The White Paper (European Commission, 2020a) refers to human dignity several times: it denotes it as one of the fundamental rights on which the EU is founded and which can be violated by the use of AI. According to the White Paper (ibid.), the international cooperation on AI matters must be based on an approach that promotes the respect of fundamental rights, including human dignity. Additionally, limitations to human dignity are listed as a potential immaterial harm of the use of AI.

As we can see, the EU documents on AI are not consistent when mentioning 'human dignity' and 'respect for human dignity'. It is not clear whether the EU defines human dignity as both an intrinsic worth of human being as well as the respect for human dignity as a fundamental right. It is also not clear whether the EU defines 'respect for human dignity' either as a fundamental right, value, or principle.

Lock (2019) explains that a famous use of the term 'principle' is made by Dworkin, who distinguishes principles from rules whereas rules apply in an all-or-nothing fashion – resulting in their not being able to conflict if both rules are to be valid, principles do not spell out the legal consequences that follow automatically when their conditions are met (see Dworkin, 1977). While it could be true that all Charter principles also happen to be Dworkinian principles, it is not true that all Charter rights are Dworkinian rules: most do not apply in an all-or-nothing fashion, but the question of whether they are violated depends on other factors, for example, whether the essence of the rights has been affected or whether a derogation is proportionate or not (Lock, 2019). This is especially true for (realised) human dignity.

Robert Alexy created the theory of constitutional rights as principles that are qualitatively different from rules, being optimisation requirements relative to what is factually and legally possible; human rights are subsumed under constitutional rights that he refers to (see Alexy, 2002). He empowers human rights with the capability of being a principle that is capable of applicability on various levels (Laciaková and Michalicková, 2013). However, distinctions between rights and principles suggested by legal theorists are unlikely to coincide with the rights-principles distinction positively drawn by the drafters of the Charter (Lock, 2019). Lock shows that the distinction between rights and principles is a political choice made by the drafters of the Charter, which means that it is, to an extent, arbitrary. Nonetheless, the distinction is relevant in practice as the categorisation of a Charter provision as a right or a principle determines the extent to which it is justiciable. The duties found in Charter principles are binding on the EU (and the Member States when implementing EU law) regardless of whether the principle has been implemented. Implementation is only relevant for their justiciability (ibid.). Laciaková and Michalicková (2013) state that the distinction between rights and principles in the Charter is not only unnecessary but also unacceptable because it may cause a degradation of the level of human rights protection in the European Union, based on the theory of constitutional rights as principles, created by Robert Alexy.

Relying either on the distinctions between rights and principles suggested by legal theorists or the one drawn by the drafters of the Charter, we could define human dignity as a fundamental right and/or principle only when referring to the dimension of realised dignity (or 'respect for human dignity' as named by the Charter). In contrast, initial dignity should not be regarded as a fundamental right and/or principle, as explained by Kleindienst (2016). For example, initial dignity when being considered as a legal principle would be subject to a weighing process, when in conflict with other legal principles. In this case, some other legal principles may weigh over the initial dignity. The described understanding of initial dignity in terms of a legal principle clearly contradicts the basic definition of this dimension of human dignity. As explained in the previous chapters, initial dignity is an inherent human characteristic that cannot be changed under any circumstances in which a person finds themselves. It is inseparably linked to human beings and is universal; it exists in any space and time and cannot be limited or diminished. If we define initial dignity as a legal principle, its scope could be diminished in favour of other legal principles. In such cases, the initial dignity could not be recognised as human essence, and thus it could no longer be interpreted as a constitutive element of man (ibid.). Therefore, we believe that initial dignity, in contrast to the realised dignity, cannot be defined as a legal principle.

Furthermore, in contrast to realised dignity, initial dignity cannot be defined as a value. For the purpose of this chapter, we refer to the conceptualisation of values according to Deth and Scarbough (2004). Thereby, we interpret the values as conceptions of desirability. Initial dignity, defined as a value, would represent the goal or motive that we want to achieve and that directs the individual's behaviour and relations among people. However, initial dignity in itself exists as a metaphysical characteristic, regardless of human interactions with the world. It indicates the status of an absolute intrinsic value, which is bound to the human being. Thus, we cannot characterise it as merely a conception of desirability (see Kleindienst, 2016) as it cannot represent merely a goal for which we are striving or an ideal we are attempting to approach. Rather, it represents an existing value related to the fact that one belongs to the human species. In contrast, realised dignity ('respect for human dignity') can be defined as a value since it represents a goal to which we are striving. Additionally, as realised dignity can be violated and diminished, it perfectly fits into the scope of values.

4. Conclusion

This chapter showed that EU documents on AI frequently rely on human dignity. However, definitions and interpretations of human dignity are relatively confusing in these documents. The rights-principles distinction drawn by the drafters of the Charter is not consistent with rights-principles distinctions suggested by legal theorists. Additionally, in contrast to realised dignity (i.e., 'respect for human dignity' as named by the Charter), initial dignity (i.e., 'intrinsic worth' as named by the Charter) should not be defined as a right and/or principle. However, as AI HLEG states, 'respect for human dignity' involves a recognition of the inherent value of humans, meaning the recognition of initial dignity. Only realised dignity could be potentially defined as a principle as well as value. Therefore, when describing human dignity in EU strategies and policies, we suggest relying on the definitions of the legal terms 'fundamental rights', 'principles', and 'values' as set by the key legal authors. Referring to human dignity either as a fundamental right, principle, or value should not be subject to arbitrary choice. Instead, the interpretation of human dignity should take into consideration the definitions of the key legal terms. Consistency and transparency are not needed only throughout the different policies and strategic goals but also throughout their retention to assure the set goal (Pandiloska Jurak, 2019, 116).

According to EU documents on AI, a common foundation of fundamental rights is rooted in respect for human dignity. This interpretation is in line with Kant's writings about the need to respect a human being which suggests that a person should be considered as an objective and never as a means. As Kleindienst explains (2017), when taking the concept of human dignity into account, Kant's following practical imperative can be applied: 'Act so that you use humanity, as much in your own person as in the person of every other, always at the same time as end and never merely as means' (Kant, 1785). This is often called the 'dignity principle' or the 'principle of humanity' (Monteiro, 2014).

Ethics Guidelines for Trustworthy AI (AI HLEG, 2019) are relatively advanced in considering human dignity in a comprehensive manner. Despite the inconsistency in defining human dignity, as described in this chapter, Ethics Guidelines for Trustworthy AI imply recognition of both initial and realised dignity, meaning consideration of human dignity in a relatively comprehensive manner. However, all the other EU policies and strategies mentioned in this chapter refer to human dignity merely superficially, mainly only in relation to the realised dignity. Thus, we suggest more consistent and encompassing consideration of the human dignity concept in EU strategies and policies, taking into consideration both dimensions of human dignity. As Kleindienst and Tomšič (2017) explain, the relationship between institutional systems and cultural platforms of society is mutually reinforcing. In this context, it is crucial to rely on the human dignity concept in a comprehensive manner: considering that human dignity is a two-dimensional concept that consists of initial and realised dignity. If EU strategies and policies do not align to both dimensions of human dignity, the relevance of this concept could be significantly hampered in the eyes of EU citizens. Additionally, such a situation can lead to flat-rate references to human dignity that do not reflect the relevance of this concept.

References

Ahmet, Christina, Artificial Intelligence: How Advanced Machine Learning Will Shape the Future of Our World (Shockwave Publishing, 2018).

AI HLEG (High-Level Expert Group on Artificial Intelligence), Ethics Guidelines for Trustworthy AI (2019), European Commission, <https://ec.europa.eu/futurium/en/ai-alliance-consultation/guidelines#Top>, accessed 1 April 2019.

Alexy, Robert, A Theory of Constitutional Rights (Oxford, New York, Frankfurrt: Oxford University Press, 2002).

Arelli, Sridhar Goud, Artificial Intelligence: The Future Way of Technology (Independently Published, 2018).

Aquinas, Thomas, Summa Theologica (New York: Benziger Brothers, 1947).

Barak, Aharon, Human Dignity, The Constitutional Value and the Constitutional Right (Cambridge: Cambridge University Press, 2015).

Beckert, Jens, 'How Do Fields Change? The Interrelations of Institutions, Networks, and Cognition in the Dynamics of Markets', Organization Studies 31 (2010), 605–627, doi: 10.1177/0170840610372184.

Capps, Patrick, Human Dignity and the Foundations of International Law (Oxford: Hart Publishing, 2009).

Cath, Corinne, Sandra Wachter, Brent Mittelstadt, Mariarosaria Taddeo and Luciano Floridi, 'Artificial Intelligence and the "Good Society": The US, EU, and UK Approach', Sci Eng Ethics 24 (2018), 505–528, doi: 10.1007/s11948-017-9901-7.

Cicero, Marcus Tullius, De officiis, tran. by Walter Miller (London: William Heinemann, 1913).

Council of Europe, 'Algorithms and Human Rights, Study on the human rights dimensions of automated data processing techniques and possible regulatory implications' (2018). <https://rm.coe.int/algorithms-and-human-rights-en-rev/16807956b5>, accessed 1 April 2020.

Deth, Jan W. van and Scarbrough, Elinor, 'The Concept of Values'. In: Jan W. van Deth and Elinor Scarbrough (eds.), The Impact of Values (Oxford: Oxford University Press, 2004), 21–47.

Donnelly, Jack, Universal Human Rights in Theory and Practice (New York: Cornell University Press, 2013).

Dupré, Catherine, The Age of Dignity: Human Rights and Constitutionalism in Europe (Oxford and Portland, Oregon: Hart Publishing, 2015).

Dworkin, Ronald, Taking Rights Seriously (London: Duckworth, 1977).

European Commission, Artificial Intelligence for Europe (2018a), SWD(2018) 137 final.

European Commission, 'Communication on Enabling the digital transformation of health and care in the Digital Single Market; empowering citizens and building a healthier society' (2018b), COM(2018) 233 final.

European Commission, 'The European Green Deal' (2019a), COM(2019) 640 final, <https://eur-lex.europa.eu/legal-content/EN/TXT/?uri=COM%3A2019%3A640%3AFIN>, accessed 1 April 2020.

European Commission, 'Communication from the commission to the European Parliament, the Council, the European economic and social committee and the committee of the regions. Building Trust in Human-Centric Artificial Intelligence' (2019b), COM(2019) 168 final.

European Commission, 'White Paper "On Artificial Intelligence – A European approach to excellence and trust"' (2020a), COM(2020) 65 final, <https://ec.europa.eu/info/sites/info/files/commission-white-paper-artificial-intelligence-feb2020_en.pdf>, accessed 1 April 2020.

European Commission, 'A European strategy for data' (2020b), COM(2020) 66 final, <https://ec.europa.eu/info/sites/info/files/communication-european-strategy-data-19feb2020_en.pdf>, accessed 1 April 2020.

Flasiński, Mariusz, Introduction to Artificial Intelligence (Springer International Publishing, 2017).

Formosa, Paul in Catriona Mackenzie, 'Nussbaum, Kant, and the Capabilities Approach to Dignity', Ethical Theory and Moral Practice (2014), January: 1–18, doi: 10.1007/s10677-014-9487-y.

Fosch-Villaronga, Eduard, Robots, Healthcare, and the Law: Regulating Automation in Personal Care (London and New York: Routledge, 2019).

Gastmans, Chris in Jan De Lepeleire, 'Living to the Bitter End? A Personalist Approach to Euthanasia in Persons with Severe Dementia', Bioethics 24/2 (2010), 78–86. doi: 10.1111/j.1467-8519.2008.00708.x.

Gilabert, Pablo, Human Dignity and Human Rights (Oxford: Oxford University Press, 2018).

Harris, Michael C., Artificial Intelligence (Marshall Cavendish Benchmark, 2011).

Golob, Tea, 'Exploring Identifications in the Transnational Social Sphere: The Potential of Social Fields', Sociologija i prostor: časopis za istraživanje prostornog i sociokulturnog razvoja 52/2 (199) (2014), 123–140.

Golob, Tea, 'Notranji dialog, refleksivnost in odgovorno delovanje mladih = Internal dialogue, reflexivity, and responsible behavior of the young', Phainomena: glasilo Fenomenološkega društva v Ljubljani 29 (114/115) (2020), 193–222, doi: 10.32022/PHI29.2020.114-115.9.

Golob, Tea, Sebastjan Kristovič and Matej Makarovič, 'European Transnational Social Fields and Identifications: The Significance of Transnational Participation and Structured Positions in the Individual and National Context', European Journal of Science and Theology 10/5 (2014), 1–20.

Kant, Immanuel, Groundwork for the Metaphysics of Moral, tran. and ed. By Allen W. Wood (New Heaven: Yale University Press, 2002 [1785]).

Kanuck, Sean, 'Humor, Ethics, and Dignity: Being Human in the Age of Artificial Intelligence', Ethics & International Affairs 33/1 (2019), 3–12.

Kateb, George, Human Dignity (Cambridge, MA: The Belknap Press, 2011).

Kleindienst, Petra, 'The Nature of Human Dignity', Research and Discussions 9/1–3 (2016), 195–232.

Kleindienst, Petra, 'Understanding the Different Dimensions of Human Dignity: Analysis of the Decision of the Constitutional Court of the Republic of Slovenia on the "Tito Street" Case', DANUBE: Law and Economics Review 8/3 (2017), 117–137.

Kleindienst, Petra, 'Vloga izobraževalnega sistema pri razvoju demokratične politične kulture', Doktorska disertacija (Fakulteta za uporabne družbene študije v Novi Gorici, 2018).

Kleindienst, Petra, 'Zgodovinski temelji sodobne paradigme človekovega dostojanstva', Phainomena: glasilo Fenomenološkega društva v Ljubljani 28/108–109 (2019), 259–282.

Kleindienst, Petra and Matevž Tomšič, 'Human Dignity as the Foundation of Democratic Political Culture: Legal and Philosophical Perspective', Law, Culture and the Humanities, 1–20 (2017), doi: 10.177/143872117738229.

Korsgaard, Christine M., Creating the Kingdom of Ends (New York: Cambridge University Press, 1996).

Laciaková, Veronika and Jana Michalicková, 'Rights and Principles – Is There a Need to Distinguish Them in the Charter of Fundamental Rights of the European Union?', Contemporary Readings in Law and Social Justice 5/2 (2013).

Leroux, Cristophe and Roberto Labruto, Ethical Legal and Societal issues in robotics, euRobotics The European Robotics Coordination, Action (2012), <https://www.researchgate.net/profile/Christophe_Leroux/publication/310167726_Ethical_Legal_and_Societal_issues_in_robotics/links/5829f77008ae138f1bf2fe4b.pdf>, accessed 1 April 2020.

Lock, Tobias, 'Rights and Principles in the EU Charter of Fundamental Rights', Common Market Law Review (2019), <https://ssrn.com/abstract=3447798>, accessed 1 April 2020.

Mahmoudi, Hoda and Michael L. Penn, Interdisciplinary Perspectives on Human Dignity and Human Rights (Bingley, UK: Emerald Publishing Limited, 2020).

Makarovič, Matej and Tea Golob, 'Increasing Fluidity of Identifications in the Context of Individualisation: Identification with the European Union', International Social Science Journal (2015), 1–13.

Makarovič, Matej, Janez Šušteršič and Borut Rončević, 'Is Europe 2020 Set to Fail?: The Cultural Political Economy of the EU Grand Strategies. European Planning Studies, 22/3 (2014), 610–626.

McCrudden, Christopher, ed., 'Understanding Human Dignity', Proceedings of the British Academy (Oxford: Oxford University Press, 2013).

Modic, Dolores and Borut Rončević, 'Social Topography for Sustainable Innovation Policy: Putting Institutions, Social Networks and Cognitive Frames in Their Place', Comparative Sociology, 17(1) (2018), 100–127.

Monteiro, A. Reis, Ethics of Human Rights (Heidleberg, New York, Dordrecht, London: Springer International Publishing, 2014).

Moore, George Edward, Principia Ethica (Cambridge: Cambridge University Press, 1903).

Pandiloska Jurak, Alenka, 'Public Policy Instrument Evaluation in Service of Enabling Grand Strategy Discourse: Case of Horizon 2020 Key Indicators', Research in Social Change, 11/2 (2019), 97–121. doi:10.2478/rsc-2019-0011.

Pico della Mirandola, Giovanni, O človekovem dostojanstvu, tran. by Brane Senegačnik (Ljubljana: Družina, 1997 [1496]).

Rončević, Borut, 'Regional development agencies and changing social fields: Towards a sociology of regional systems of innovation'. In: Bellini, Nicola, Mike Danson and Henrik Halkier (eds.), Regional Development Agencies: The Next Generation?: Networking, Knowledge and Regional Policies (London; New York: Routledge, 2012), 87–101.

Rončević, Borut, 'Technology and Innovations in Regional Development for Europe 2020: Jean Monnet Centre of Excellence TIR 2020 for Smart, Inclusive and Sustainable Growth', Research in Social Change, 12/3 (2020), 5–14.

Rončević, Borut and Dolores Modic, 'Regional Systems of Innovations as Social Fields'. Sociologija i prostor: časopis za istraživanje prostornoga i sociokulturnog razvoja, 49/191 (2011), 313–333.

Rončević, Borut and Dolores Modic, 'Social fields of technological innovations'. In: Nikolai Genov (ed.), Global Trends and Regional Development (New York: Routledge, 2012), 226–247.

Rončević, Borut and Matevž Tomšič, 'Perspectives of information society: Bricolage of manifestations'. In: Rončević, Borut and Matevž Tomšič (eds.) Information Society and Its Manifestations: Economy, Politics, Culture (Frankfurt am Main: Peter Lang, 2017), 9–21.

Rončević, Borut and Tamara Besednjak Valič, 'How to Think about Regional Development Agencies as a Sociologist'. The Social Sciences, 14/9 (2019), 326–334.

Rončević, Borut, Matej Makarovič, Matevž Tomšič and Victor Cepoi, 'Methodological solutions for comparative research on transformations'. In: P. Vihalemm, A. Masso, and S. Opermann (eds.) The Routledge International Handbook of European Social Transformations (Abingdon and New York: Routledge, 2018), 57–70.

Rosen, Michael, Dignity, Its History and Meaning (Cambridge, MA/ London: Harvard University Press, 2012).

Sensen, Oliver, 'Human Dignity in Historical Perspective: The Contemporary and Traditional Paradigms', European Journal of Political Theory 10/1 (2011), 71–91.

Sharkey, Amanda, 'Robots and human dignity: A Consideration of the Effects of Robot Care on the Dignity of Older People', Ethics and Information Technology, 16/1 (2014), 63–75.

Shultziner, Doron, 'Human Dignity – Functions and Meanings', Global Jurists Topics, 3/3 (2003), 1–21.

Sulmasy, Daniel P., 'Dignity and Bioethics: History, Theory, and Selected Applications'. In Adam Schulman and Thomas W. Merrill (eds.), Human Dignity and Bioethics: Essays Commissioned by the President's Council on Bioethics, (Washington, DC: Government Printing Office, 2008), Chapter 18.

Vallor, Shannon, 'Carebots and Caregivers: Sustaining the Ethical Ideal of Care in the Twenty-First Century', Philosophy & Technology 24/3 (2011), 251.

Waldron, Jeremy, 'Is Dignity the Foundation of Human Rights?', Public Law and Legal Theory Paper Series (New York University, School of Law, 2013), 12–73.

Wood, Allen W., Kant's Ethical Thought (Cambridge: Cambridge University Press, 1999).

Zardiashvili, L., and Fosch-Villaronga, E., 'Oh, Dignity Too? Said the Robot: Human Dignity as the Basis for the Governance of Robotics', Minds & Machines, <https://doi.org/10.1007/s11023-019-09514-6>, accessed 1 April 2020.

Cristian Gangaliuc

Clusters vs Networks: A Dilemma for Regional Innovation Policy

Abstract: Apart from empirical observations and expertise, public policy often comes to be influenced by academic research's theoretical frameworks and models. The same is true for the formulation of regional innovation policy. In this regard, the article considers two different developmental models – the industrial agglomeration and social integration paradigms – presenting their potential inputs for regional innovation strategy. Highlighting the cluster and network concepts, the paper concludes by acknowledging the importance of information creation and diffusion and the relevance of the type of information for planning and implementation of policy.

Keywords: Public policy, innovation, networks, clusters, Regional Innovation System, open innovation, development

1. Introduction

It has been established that the competitive advantages of regions and nations do not predominantly rely on the capacity to increase the supply factors, but rather to gain more and better outputs from the input resources (Porter, 1990; Rosenberg, 2004). Multiple examples, like Japan and Korea's economic 'miracles', were directly linked to the efforts of catching up with and overtaking more developed nations due to modernisation of production and products (Porter, 1990; Sohn and Kenney, 2007). Examples like these showed the need to increase innovativeness so that national, supra-national, and sub-national entities could maintain their competitiveness. It resulted in various innovation policies ranging from corporate/firm management to regional, national, and even international public strategies.

The European Union (EU) has developed a strong sense of importance and awareness for the necessity to promote and support innovative growth in its grand strategies (Makarovič et al., 2014). The EU's developmental priorities for 2020 (European Commission, 2010) emphasised the smart specialisation strategies with innovation as one of the crucial tools for achieving the goal. The subject of innovation appeared on the list of priorities for Europe's future and was included in the strategic vision for 2030 (European Commission, 2019). It emphasises the necessity of achieving sustainable growth as a means of transition to a circular and green economy and dealing with regional developmental discrepancies. In this context, it is relevant that EU strategies and policies follow the main values that the EU is based upon, for example, human dignity as the leading EU principle (Kleindienst, 2017, 2019; Kleindienst and Tomšič, 2017; Kleindienst and Tomšič, 2018).

To emphasise the importance of the discourse on innovation, the EU's implementation of priorities was realised on various levels and through different mechanisms. The direct approach was the promotion of national policies to achieve economic developments and invest in innovative projects and practices. However, the direct means were not successful enough in various contexts and regions (European Commission, 2019). In this regard, innovation and developmental projects were 'subcontracted' to the civil society and social institutions through the Erasmus+, Horizon, Interreg and other funded projects, with the intention of supporting bottom-top developmental strategies. Multiple actors, as higher education institutions (HEI), administrative bodies, support organisations and institutions, small and developed business were contributing with their vision and expertise to increase the innovative capacity of Europe.

The EU quest for specialisation, transition to a green and circular economy (Fric et al., 2020; Fric and Roncevic, 2018, 2020; Roncevic and Fric, 2015; Džajić Uršič and Rončević, 2017; Mileva Boshkoska et al., 2018) and development indicates that the necessity for smart innovation policy, planning, and strategy is highly relevant (e.g., Besednjak Valic, 2019). That leads to the question of the adequate approach to policy development and implementation processes. As it is not only an empirically-based process but also theory-influenced, the importance of assumptions and approaches, borrowed from academic society and their models, are also affecting the way in which the strategies are written and carried out (e.g., Uyarra, 2010, Rončević, 2019). In this regard, explanatory theories, models, and paradigms of innovation have a major role and motivate different planning and action frames.

Among all theories on development and innovation that affected the policy debate, co-locational and networks paradigms attracted many supporters and developed strong argumentative bodies (Uyarra, 2010). Using Granovetter's (1985) terminology, the spatial agglomeration approach (Porter, 1990) can be called an 'under-socialised' model, emphasising the value of actors (industries and companies) being closely located for their ability to enhance competitiveness. In contrast, the network model (Cooke, 1992; Chesbrough, 2003) falls into the area of 'over-socialised' paradigms, considering that in order to handle innovativeness, enterprises should be socially and economically interconnected.

Relatively similar but significantly different, both theories provided a great deal of room for policy formulation and implementation. Both explanatory designs have their reliable positions as well as assumptive flows, but none was capable of performing an elaborated explication to satisfy all the critique. It is necessary to pay special attention to the selection of a model, to examine the potential results and find possible solutions to correct deficiencies (e.g., Pandiloska Jurak and Pinterič, 2012).

The absence of consensus upon the definition of an industrial cluster (Pratt, 2004), and the unsettled debate between supporters of over-socialised and under-socialised models, raises new ambiguity for policy formulation. Even after three decades of research, there is still some ambivalent area about the full potential of geographical proximity and social links (Brenner et al., 2011). Moreover, the complexity of methodological assessment of innovation (e.g. Gangaliuc, 2019), issues with policy indicators (e.g. Pandiloska Jurak, 2019), and conceptual fuzziness of networks and geographical externalities add to the sophistication of policy decision-making processes (Brenner et al., 2011).

Empirical actions, based on these paradigms, would also carry vague definitions and categorisations. In this regard, the paper proposes briefly reviewing both theoretical frameworks and considering their potential and added value for policy planning, formulation and implementation. The main focus is to highlight theoretical models, conceptual variables and explanatory designs regarding innovation, especially for regional innovation strategy. In parallel, try to identify similarities and main differences of listed approaches to capture potential common ground.

2. Cluster, Specialisation and Innovativeness: How Does It Work?

Porter's work on national economic development (1990) is considered a relevant contribution to the literature on innovation. In Porter's view, the competitive advantage gained by a nation is based upon the interdependence of four factors: (1) National Infrastructure (including workforce skills); (2) Competitive Pressure of (Local) Industries; (3) The Role of Inter-Industrial Support; and (4) The Governance System of Businesses. All these factors are interconnected and create cardinal points of the 'Diamond of National Advantage' (Porter, 1990). The description of each of the four factors and the nature of the phenomena they represent lead to the conclusion that each is spatially limited or has a finite area of effect. Thus, Porter's argument establishes that National Advantage Diamonds create locations where economies thrive. This

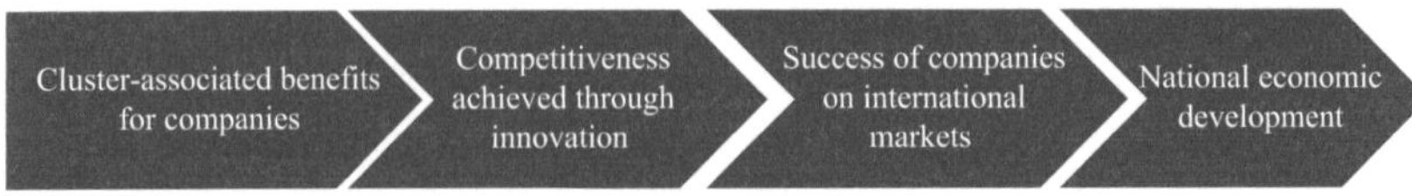

Fig. 1: From clusters to national economic development
Source: Author's interpretation.

stimulates an agglomeration of industries 'connected by specialised buyer-supplier relationships or related by technologies or skills' (Porter, 1996: 85), characterised by local competition and specialised demand, further defined as a Cluster. In his view, clusters are dynamic entities with the capacity to learn, change and adapt, in order to modernise and evolve (Porter, 1990, 1996). The agglomeration paradigm considers that companies' natural necessity to innovate and gain competitive advantage (that shall match the rate of rivals catching up), could drive their interest to join or create clusters, rather than remain atomised players (Furman, Porter and Stern, 2002). It allows enterprises to benefit from their improved capacity to diffuse and create value, assuming a critical role for co-location and its associated externalities in the process of innovation. Summarily, Porter's work can be illustrated within a simple logical chain (Fig. 1):

The cluster paradigm argues that the framework for development and improvements in co-located industries lies within the firm's capacity to communicate and react to environmental impulses (Furman, Porter and Stern, 2001). The latter could include the 'set of pressures' (competitive, peer, and customer pressures), constant comparison among organisations, quality of linkages between companies, the roles of universities, common technological infrastructure, and others (Porter, 1990, 1996; Furman, Porter and Stern, 2001; Pratt, 2004).

Impulses and communication create a bipolar view on the role of competitiveness within the cluster paradigm. On the one hand, they argue that companies gain initiatives for innovation by creating competitive pressure; on the other, they assume that rival companies are more likely to communicate and associate (probably even unconscious) within clusters. Such 'quasi-competitiveness' allows companies to sustain a decent level of pressure to support the competitive status quo while allowing them to collaborate for common benefit. As a result, companies in industrial agglomerations have increased capacity for progress and development, and the region itself prospers and maintains competitive stature on international markets, even if some enterprises fall behind

(Furman, Porter and Stern, 2001). Thus, theoretically, spatial proximity creates an atmosphere of information dissemination and genuine motivation for performance.

Complementary to Porter's work, other relevant explanations and externalities were attributed to the spatial agglomeration. Some researchers argued that geographically close companies rely on decreased costs of transactions and transportation (Capello, 2011; Insead et al., 2005; Pratt, 2004), lower decisional costs (Insead et al., 2005), increased degree of specialisation (Doloreux and Parto, 2005; Romanielli and Khessina, 2005), untraded places-specific interactions, including communication and product standardisation (Porter, 1990; Pratt, 2004; Insead et al., 2005) and support from trust and inter-firm reputation (Parto, 2008). These determinants and externalities are of both dynamic and static character. The fixed ones are directly linked to the facts of geographical proximity, like transportation costs or place-specific interactions. Others are consequent to change and continuous communication among enterprises, like the specialisation and standardisation of cluster products.

In this regard, the agglomeration proves to be related not only to concrete spatial proximity, but maybe even more so, to the information exchange. In the case of closely placed actors, the impact of communication increases with the frequency of them performing face-to-face meetings (both formal and accidental) (Lazzarini, Miller and Zenger, 2008; Schoales, 2006; Golob 2014; Golob and Makarovič 2018). This kind of 'untraded' externalities (Rocha and Stenrberg, 2005) provides advantages to cluster firms and fosters their common strategy and innovativeness. In time, among agents that benefit from the presence in a cluster, potential informational spill-overs and information exchange begin (Baptista, 2001; Hafner and Modic, 2019). Through knowledge dissemination, companies are open to perform and accept standardised qualities of products and production processes, fostering their adaptive and problem-solving capacities. This is why innovation is seen as place-specific phenomena, being determined by the characteristics of the community and their economic activities and enterprises' capacity for inter-organisational knowledge and resource flow (Doloreux and Parto, 2005). These assumptions seem aligned with European Specialisation strategies, providing explanation and potential for action. However, the theoretical framework of clusters is difficult to adapt for a regional policy. Its definition does not allow a clear understanding of the phenomenon, being applied both to companies and industries simultaneously (e.g., Porter, 1998). That makes it unclear in terms of what specialisation can mean: the co-location of same-industry companies or the presence of a group of support industries that enhance each other's capacities.

Additionally to information exchange, location provides support from universities and R&D institutes, cultural background, and regulations, which contribute to the creation and dissemination of new ideas (e.g., Doloreux and Parto, 2005; Bell 2005; Hess and Yeung, 2006; Cepoi, 2020). Innovativeness depends on the whole spectre of a community's structural factors. With information exchange, companies benefit from a pool of added knowledge and can perform analytical deductions about other companies' competitive strategies. With the overlapping of the firm's exogenous and endogenous information, enterprises are able to produce new knowledge and communicate it to other members of the cluster (Tallman, Jenkins and Pinch, 2004). Similarly, institutions and support organisations are part of this process, by providing new knowledge, links and, through legislation, directly and indirectly regulating these processes (Bell, 2005; Doloreux and Parto, 2005). For the under-socialised paradigm, cultural and institutional 'developmental reagents' are rooted in the location. Thus, summing up the arguments, and acknowledging the static and dynamic factors of innovation, allows them to conclude that innovation is a place-specific phenomenon (Doloreux and Parto, 2005).

2.1 The Matter of Specialisation

As a developmental priority of the EU and its Member States, this topic requires a separate analysis and explanation. Within the industrial agglomeration paradigm, it touches the issue of standardisation and quality assurance as potentially influencing the development and modernisation rates (Porter, 1990, 1996; Insead et al., 2005; Romanielli and Khessina, 2005; Giuliani, Piertobelli and Rabelloti, 2005).

Considering the cluster theory and the Diamond of National Advantage, specialisation is necessary for a cluster to develop. By providing exclusive production and serving specialised local demands, regions begin to attract particular resources and skills (e.g., capable and appropriate workforce), deepening the degree of production and product specialisation (Porter, 1990, 1996; Romaneli and Khessina, 2005; Parto, 2008; Feser and Bergman, 2000). Moreover, the migration of employees among cluster firms became another spatial factor that enhances information diffusion and adds to the degree of specialisation (Giuliani, Piertobelli and Rabelloti, 2005; Parto, 2008; Feser and Bergman, 2000; Pratt, 2004). In such a context, the information that flows within a cluster becomes place-specific, concerning local/regional industries and economic agents' needs and particularities. The specialised information becomes obsolete for the non-cluster members, or at least its importance fades with the distance (Bell, 2005; Pratt, 2004; Baptista, 2001). However, recent theories provide stronger support for cluster information as being beneficial to outsiders. Strategic coupling process is based on the principle of specialised skills and knowledge, contradicting the early views (e.g., Yeung, 2009, 2015).

A concentration of information of a specific type and character is a double-edged sword. On the one hand, it creates pools of knowledge where information can be used for continuous development. It allows companies to gain added value from the shared know-how and to build upon the existing knowledge and spread more added value. Such, -learning by doing- logic (Parto, 2008) enables the creation of certain pools of skills, resources, technology and workforce that can easily interact and combine, showing strong supportive capacity. On the other hand, it increases the risk of overspecialisation or over-embeddedness (Uzzi, 1996), further eroding the quality of cooperation for engaged parties. Similarly, relying only on regional information endangers regional development and reduces its competences to learn from foreign examples and even follow the global trends of industries (Bathelt, Malmberg and Maskell, 2004; Yeung, 2015). It indicates that a cluster can provide a necessary boost and support for innovation; however, it is not entirely capable of compensating for all the required components.

2.2 Ability to Mimic

Another topic of relevance to the industrial agglomeration paradigm is the concept of mimicry (Porter, 1990; Insead et al., 2005; Bel, 2005). In close proximity, an important factor is the capacity of observation. The fact that it does not require a direct link with another actor, and can be performed without any interactions (Bell, 2005), makes this concept unique. It provides an alternative source of knowledge that can be used for innovative combinations. Mimicry allows firms to copy someone's decision and, in the implementation process, trigger unique changes, leading to originality and consolidation of their innovative performance (Bell, 2005).

Following the cluster paradigm, mimicry is presented as reducing the decision-making costs, attending competitive necessities, or being forced to act through non-competitive social or economic factors (Insead et al., 2005). For the first part, each administrative or technological transformation comes with certain market-performance risks. Thus, when a certain company implements an innovative decision, it encourages others to be open to the change and aware of the potential final results, reducing the tension of decision-making. In a situation of uncertainty, enterprises could copy a decision to legitimise personal actions, thus reducing managerial pressure. Similarly, in a competitive struggle, firms could mimic a certain market adversary, as insurance for not 'falling behind' and maintain market status-quo. It makes it a rather necessary decision than a voluntary one.

The last explanations derive from the cultural and social norms of regional communities. Alternatively, it can be found in psychological and cultural group affiliation, implying that performing a copy-paste step is just a way to 'fall in line'. Nonetheless, empirical evidence shows that copying someone's actions has a limited effect on firms (Baptista, 2001; Modic and Roncevic, 2018). It is clear that non-action is risky; thus mimicry of a successful performance seems reasonable. However, several sets of issues surround the matter. Certain transformations do not necessarily combine with firm day-by-day routine, making mimicry obsolete or even dangerous for the adopter. Moreover, the innovative value of copying a decision decreases with the number of actors that implemented the change (Baptista, 2001), making it a vain effort if the companies are late adopters.

Close spatial location brings interdependent and indirect externalities, allowing companies to benefit from easy access to information and knowledge (Baptista, 2001) – to use Marshal's metaphor: the information 'in the air' (Tallman, Jenkins and Pinch, 2004; Bell, 2005). Similarly, geographical agglomeration allows cluster enterprises to perform direct observations of closest neighbours (Insead et al., 2005), thus increasing their chances to maintain an adequate appraisal of the necessary actions they require for innovation and development. It builds upon the necessity to centralise and group the economic actors in the same space without neglecting the social factors (resembling supportive forces). Mainly, the argument suggests that innovativeness is merely a process of local actors, that due to their proximity began to interact (not necessarily intentionally), encouraging technological and administrative development. Unmistakably, it has multiple implications for policy formulation and implementation.

3. Networks and Socio-Institutional Integration Model

Similar in certain aspects but different in interpretation of social and geographical factors is the network paradigm. Some are even discussing 'networkisation' in the information society (Rončević and Tomšič). As in the cluster model, information exchange is the key factor of innovativeness (Asheim and Coenen, 2005; Grabher, 2006). The over-socialised theory emphasises that social interactions create the necessary condition for cohesion and information flow. That induces the important point of difference of approaches towards the actor's participation in information exchange. For closely located players, it is a matter of context (being in the area) that determines the access to the knowledge pool, while for network theory, it is the conscious association with the group.

Granovetter's (1985) work on embeddedness was one of the first mentions on the network's added value, researching the importance of 'weak ties' for a person's economic advantages. Although his paper reflects on factors helping with employment, economists and sociologists adopted his vision for a wider, market-related, economic activity of companies (e.g., Uzzi, 1996; Asheim and Coenen, 2005; Lazarinni, Miller and Zenger, 2008). The importance of connections and the building of ties presented itself as a complex concept with various explanations and models for development and innovativeness. It can be developed from the standpoint of interactions of larger groups and multiple types of actors, as in Regional Innovation Systems (e.g., Cooke, 2000). Similarly, it can be assessed as a theory explaining the utility of ties for a node in the network by promoting open collaboration and communication (e.g., Chesbrough, 2003).

3.1 Regional Innovation System and Open Innovation Theories

Cooke's (1992, 2001) model of Regional Innovation System (RIS) captures some aspects similar to Porter's cluster design on the level of regional importance and policy planning. The focus is on fostering communication (Asheim and Coenen, 2005), or in Cooke's (1992) words: 'learning through interaction'. Nonetheless, these are not hazardous ties; knowledge creation and dissemination are rooted in 'learning through networking' (Cooke, 1992: 381). To explain: RIS theory considers the success of Wales' enterprises and its diverse innovative programmes. In the case study, the success lies in the capacity to establish communication among various stakeholders. Additionally, important supportive factors are the connectivity circumstances, such as investment in R&D processes, private and public industry support, specialised and highly qualified technological market and skills and, above all, enterprises' attitude toward innovation (Cooke, 1992).

In this context, Cooke does not neglect the fact that co-location plays an important role, allowing firms to benefit from well-known reputation, expectations and capabilities of neighbouring enterprises and institutions (Cooke, 2001). That explicitly shows the fundamental difference between cluster and network theories. RIS investigates innovation from the point-of-view of group-interactions, which includes the ability to decide their group-synergy level, while in co-location theories that was an almost-pre-established fact, due to the existence of communication. Even so, it is wrong to assume that Porter's model is completely related to situational element, leaving firms to 'fate', and that RIS treats them as conscious players with complete control over the situation. It is rather a mix of both, and the difference being the contrast of the roles attributed to locational externalities and social-economic ties. In networks, the governance principles are distinct factors of innovativeness (West et al., 2014). Organisational capacity and co-operative strategies, as elements of governance, are individual for each group. In other words, it assumes path-dependent evolution (Rončević and Makarovič, 2010, 2011; Rončević and Fric, 2017), attributing for each network a unique capacity to innovate (Modic and Rončević, 2018; Erman, 2020).

Moving to a more actor-driven explanation, the Open Innovation (OI) paradigm (Chesbrough, 2003; West et al., 2014) also reflects on the role of network for the processes of technological and managerial development. OI suggests that innovativeness and learning are not exclusively internal processes but rather depend on the firm's external exchange of information and degree of collaboration. In such a context, group inter-exchange becomes a decisive factor for a firm's innovativeness, and through it, for regions. It stipulates that innovation procedure resembles an open system, constituting horizontally embedded enterprises and supportive high-education, research and other knowledge creation institutions. It considers the same basic pylons of RIS, which are the dynamism of the systems, communication and collaboration among firms and specialised institutions, the non-hierarchical character of network links, and emphasis on enterprises' innovation culture.

Considering the examples of RIS and OI designs, the similarity between network and system is suggestive. As information and knowledge flow are crucial for innovativeness, some specific, logical conditions should be fulfilled for it to take place. Firstly, a subject should exist, and, secondly, an object of exchange, meaning between whom the transfer is ensured and what it is supposed to communicate. This is why the network, as a general concept, is fundamental. Networks ensure the existence of structure and relationships to serve as necessities for exchange. The nodes of a network become the subjects of transactions, and relationships/connections between them q43 the link through which the object of exchange passes.

Network-system comparison allows assuming that networks have similar characteristics to those of systems. More specific, structure and relationships are highly interdependent. As structure can determine the quantity, vector and members of a network, so do the links between them are capable of influencing and changing the structure. In other words, within one particular structure, a certain type of relationship exists, but once a new relationship appears, it transforms the structure.

The second major impact is that the structure of a system, especially relationships and the strength of ties, determines the quality of information that passes through them (Rocha, 2004). It was repeatedly suggested by researchers that different types of interaction are responsible for the volume and particularities of knowledge circulating through the network (Granovetter, 1985; Tallman, Jenkins and Pinch, 2004; Bathelt, Malmberg and Maskell, 2004). In that regard, internal governance of both hierarchically and horizontally embedded communities should be affected by this tandem and interactive dependency of structure and relationships (West et al., 2014; Golob and Makarovič 2017; Modic and Roncevic, 2018). It should be enough to conclude that structure and connections are fundamental parts for innovative systems.

One of the simplest examples, to consider the importance of this metaphor, is to address the issue of connectivity. Researchers consider that positioning within a network is crucial for technological development (Granovetter, 1985; Bell, 2005). The nodes with a higher number of connections would benefit from having greater chances to access new knowledge. This concept is called 'centrality', and it measures a firm's involvement in network structure (Bell, 2005). Centrality ensures some control of flowing resources, and thus, can be used to explain the difference between the innovative capacity of firms in the same network. In other words, being a fundamental part of a network allows enterprises to innovate more often. Also, by controlling the information they disseminate and the direction in which it is spread, central nodes can decide who will benefit from the information and resource diffusion (Bell, 2005). That leaves the connected node with considerably more capacity to process new knowledge and relevant information and the less associated ones to rely mostly on the information created inside the enterprise. However, it is imperative to mention that the quality of data that flow through networks should also be considered. Granovetter (1985) elaborated on how peripheral nodes could become the 'heart' of a network if they ensure diffusion of innovative and radical changes, ignored or overlooked by the old centre.

3.2 Institutions and Culture

Another conclusion that could be drawn from RIS and OI models is that institutions and cultural frames are actively present in the process of knowledge creation and distribution (e.g. Cooke, 1992; Chesbrough, 2003; Cepoi,

2016; Cepoi and Golob, 2017). Specialised institutions are key members of innovative networks that engage in the creation of non-economic and technical knowledge, with a direct impact on market capacity and competitive success for enterprises. Universities and R&D institutes are valuable providers of pools of skilled workforce and expertise, increasing specialisation and promoting firm-institution collaboration (Cooke, 1992, 2001; Etzkowitz and Klofsten, 2005). Establishing a channel of communication between universities and enterprises allows firms to be more scientifically accurate when performing or adopting innovative changes. It also ensures feedback from economic strata to R&D institutions and specialists, helping them narrow and focus their research projects to become market-oriented. Providing universities with access to technological parks increases their capacity for empirical observation and adequate assessment of research topics for economic needs.

Aside from knowledge creation and education institutions, of similar impact are economic and political institutions/organisations (Cooke, 2001; Roncevic and Besednjak Valic, 2019; Cepoi and Golob, 2016). Such entities provide innovative frameworks through supportive legislation and redistribution of resources to ensure, but preferably enhance, communication and collaboration among economic actors and with knowledge-creation organisations. The activities of political-support institutions should not be underestimated. Besides the potential for support, these organisations can also create barriers that jeopardise the whole innovative system (Beckert, 2010; Etzkowitz and Klofsten, 2005). To ensure a positive impact and expect fruitful innovative policies, these organisations should exist and evolve proportionally and interconnected with social-economic life to adapt to its needs (e.g., Cooke, 2001; Grabher, 2006; Modic and Rončević, 2018). In this regard, administrative institutions have a greater chance of becoming information providers (Bathelt, Malmberg and Maskell, 2004; Tallman, Jenkins and Pinch, 2004), helping companies survive and adapt to the economic environment. Also, on the institutional side lies the responsibility for connecting regional and international agents, as a mandatory form for the expansion of networks and potential for added value (Yeung, 2009, 2015; Rončević and Besednjak Valič, 2019). Strong institutions might serve well as guarantors for insecure transactions, temporarily substituting 'missing pieces', such as trust, reputational misunderstanding, among others. (Grabher, 2006). In other words, being transparent and allowing all the regional economic actors to benefit from information and a sustainable environment, political institutions help them overcome or benefit from different circumstances.

The informal institutions, as sociology address cultural foundations (Romanelli and Khessina, 2005), resemble the third pillar for innovativeness.

Cultural and normative arrangements, values, as well as social-interaction rules, have similar dichotomous effects. They might support and foster innovativeness or compromise its development (Doloreux and Parto, 2005; Cooke, 2001). Their direct impact affects the network itself, by providing informal regulative effect (through norms and morality) and correct what and how information is shared. This is also true for external information that penetrates the network. Cultural and cognitive frameworks determine the degree of isolation/specialisation of information absorbed by a community (Romanelli and Khessina, 2005; Doloreux and Parto, 2005; Cooke, 2001).

Moreover, cultural elements interfere with the quality of institutional frameworks, establishing the degree to which enterprises are ready to subject themselves to following political and economic regulations (Beckert, 2010; Modic and Roncevic, 2018; Besednjak Valic et al., 2020). In this context, it should be added that elements such as corruption, bureaucracy, the importance of institutionalised regulations, and similar, receive significantly less attention from researchers. Nevertheless, those could have particularly great influence, contextually providing clearance and explanatory potential.

Networks and institutional and cultural frameworks are very interdependent, sharing a set of complex relationships (Beckert, 2010; Fligstein 2001; Golob and Cepoi, 2016; Modic and Roncevic, 2018; Cepoi and Golob, 2017; Cepoi, 2019; Fric et al., 2020). Social field theory, a paradigm representing this complementary nature, considers that each network, cluster or region, is innovating and evolving according to mutual interactions between these three social forces (social networks, institutions and cognitive frames). According to social field theory, the only way to influence innovativeness is to consider that policy actions impact all three forces simultaneously (Cepoi and Golob, 2016; Cepoi, 2016; Modic and Roncevic, 2018). Beckert (2010) provides an illustrative example of such co-existence, where institutions, values and social network are presented in a cyclic figure, reinforcing each other clockwise and in the opposite directions.

There are two ways to interpret this relationship. On the one hand, networks forge the cultural and normative values, which, in turn, are transformed into legislative incentives for institutions. Until there is no resonance between network values and legislative framework, it sustains legitimacy and authority of institutions. Further, support organisations have the power to determine the structure and relationship rules of a network, influencing network subjects' behaviour. On the other hand, social webs have the power to influence institutions, making them adapt to network needs, through lobby and representativeness. That creates a precedent for policy and legislation that highlights certain existing or new values for public conduct. Thus, cultural and social norms (re)shape how networks perceive their structure and relationships, closing the cycle. Following the argument, it becomes clear that each social force has two ways to influence the other one. The first is direct, through mutual dependence among themselves and the second is indirectly, through the influence of the third factor. By adding indirect interactions and mutual dependency to the picture, social field scholars raise a valid point about the complexity of fields and methodological issues to deal with it. This is why context and path-dependency analysis are of primal value for social field scholars (e.g., Beckert, 2010; Modic and Roncevic, 2018; Roncevic et al., 2010). It leads to the conclusion that each social field has its own historical evolution process, which leads to its current developmental status. In this regard, every region – as a field – should be treated differently and approached with the understanding of its particularities. In the same context, it explains the difference in regional development, when the same input elements result in different outcomes for different regions (Cepoi and Golob, 2016).

In conclusion, the network paradigm can be viewed as a competent, alternative approach for policy formulation and development. Similar to the under-socialised model, it emphasises the role of communication and learning. Moreover, it does not neglect the importance of co-location externalities but treats them as supportive forces (e.g., Cooke, 1992, 2001; Rocha and Sternberg, 2005). Network theory can be defined as a relational model for which place is not essential (Modic and Roncevic, 2018; Ashein and Coenen, 2005). It can explain why development and innovation occur in closely knit spaces more often, while providing examples for network capacity to support development and competitiveness in companies engaged in global value chains. Nevertheless, by establishing that institutions and cognitive frames are also responsible for innovativeness, it recognises that special proximity ensures some innovative potential, because values are place-specific, as well as regulative powers of institutions (Cepoi and Golob, 2016). In other words, it is better to have a strong and efficient networking even among geographically proximate stakeholders, because co-locational externalities are seen as insufficient circumstances for innovative processes (Modic and Roncevic, 2018).

4. Information as Tool for Innovativeness

Both the over- and under-socialised theories place a focal role on knowledge and information in the context of innovation and development. It suggests the importance of data and its diffusion for the formulation and implementation of regional development policy. This opens the question of how to treat information in the context of strategy-writing and decision-making processes.

It was established that knowledge can be easy-to-access, or common information, with general, technical or non-secret data, reached through official channels or demanded from economic and political institutions. Or, it can be specific, strategic or tacit data, which is harder to come by and refers to the production and/or market-administrative factors, mainly concerning the managerial level. However, such general explanations did not cover all the complexity of knowledge and learning processes within an innovation framework.

A more in-depth description was performed by Tallman, Jenkins and Pinch (2004), differentiating information into Component Knowledge and Architectural Knowledge. Component and architectural data are similar to the concepts of common and strategic knowledge, but consider the viewpoint of enterprises and focuses on the managerial value of information. In short, component knowledge does not consider a firm as an aggregate unit; rather, it refers to separate parts of it. It answers certain questions of 'what?' and 'whom?' but is incapacitated to deal with problems like 'how?' and 'why?'. Component knowledge does not limit itself to common information, as permanently tangible and explicit. Sometimes it has a highly scientific, systemically complex and tacit character. For example, it can reflect well-known market factors, such as type of resources and supply relationships, labour contingent, and similar. In contrast, it might also be about scientific blueprints of production technology, patents, organisational routine, and similar that are usually kept hidden from external eyes. Thus, component knowledge is not only general and easy-to-access, and its dissemination depends on a firm's particular visions, complexity and exchange factors.

Architectural knowledge acts like a connection combining all the parts into a functional entity. As Tallman et al. (2004: 265) believe, it is 'integrating component knowledge into factors of production'. It is more path-dependent and reflects the historical evolution of a firm, describing its organisational essence. It is unique information, utterly accessible and comprehensible mostly by the enterprises themselves. Compared to component knowledge, it is rather complex, intangible and tacit and is treated cautiously when considering its exchange. It requires a greater amount of trust to be shared and usually is not easily reachable. Since some of its parts are uniquely relevant for the mother-company, it is harder to adapt or even incompatible for the organisational restructuring of other firms.

Tallman, Jenkins, and Pinch (2004) consider that architectural type knowledge is also applicable to cluster-level. It takes the form of firms' customary manner to coexist and collaborate. Cluster-level architectural organisation determines the behavioural model and movements patterns of information. Elaborated and complex cluster-level architectural knowledge makes it impossible for companies to hide their component information, ensuring the information flow and local information spill-overs. As this concept is similar to the Governance criteria of networks (West et al., 2014), it is reasonable to assume that information flow management and collaborative arrangements are parts of both clusters and networks, emphasising their similarity.

From another perspective, both cluster and network paradigms supposed that information is place/network specific, and the efficiency of its usage diminishes with distance, as well as its meaning (Bell, 2005; Pratt, 2004; Baptista, 2001). In this regard, Bathelt et al. (2004: 38) developed a model of companies' exogenous and endogenous communication lines, distinguishing between local-buzzes and knowledge achieved through global pipelines. According to them, local-buzz 'refers to the information and communication ecology created by face-to-face contacts, co-presence and co-location of people and firms within the same industry and place or region' (p. 38). It is similar to the architectural organisation of clusters described by Tallman, Jenkins and Pinch (2004) and Porter's (1990) example of information diffusion. Although authors consider that any information comes with certain costs, they define local communication exchange to be performed without any special or customised investments; rather, it comes naturally and is a result of accidental meetings, face-to-face interactions and shared cognitive frames. In other words, the necessary conditions are co-location and behavioural appropriation, compatible with the official and unofficial rules of the group. A defining characteristic of local buzz is the automatisation of information flow. Companies do not have to invest in or perform an additional effort to gain buzz-information; they are surrounded by it and access it easily through economic and social ties. That implies that companies are part of local buzz, even if unaware of it. Nonetheless, social or economic links determine the content of shared data. Communication will be hindered by negative effects, such as mistrust or competitive interest.

In a way, local-buzz is applicable to the theory of Social Fields. It ensures communication within networks and with institutional frames. For institutions, becoming a part of buzz ensures compatibility with market behaviour and social patterns, enhancing communication and sustaining competitiveness (Bathelt, Malmberg and Maskell, 2004). In contrast, it supports open access to local information and allows mimicry to occur, ensuring the development of the whole group. This is why many authors consider local-buzz, or similar models, to be crucial for innovation in cluster areas (Porter, 1990, 2001; Insead et al., 2005; Bell, 2005).

Nonetheless, locally embedded social ties, once growing very strong, pose a threat to innovativeness. By ignoring the dilution of information and the variety of informants, a closed system risks becoming saturated, less flexible and addicted to certain information patterns (Bathelt, Malmberg and Maskell, 2004; Etzkowitz and Klofsten, 2005; Uzzi, 1996). Basically, it is Uzzi's (1996) concept of over-embeddedness that dictates the erosive capacity of long and strong relationships. The concept explains the degenerative evolution of network links. Its main theme is that reliance on the same ties for too long marks a decrease in transactional (both financial and information) values for both edges of the link. The explanation is that by maintaining a highly embedded network, companies decrease their adaptive levels to engage in new links and adapt to new market information. Companies' trust in existing social ties, multiplied by market uncertainty, dictates continuing transactions within the same network, even if disconnection and involvement in new links would prove beneficial (Lazzarini et al., 2008). It also corrupts the general trust of nodes toward other actors on the market, decreasing the probability of engaging in new relationships (Uzzi, 1996; Wicks et al., 1999; Lazzarini et al., 2008).

In order to minimise the risk of over-embeddedness, Bathelt, Malmberg, and Maskell (2004) suggest the necessity to build external channels of communication. 'Global pipelines' provide exogenous and original knowledge that is radically different from information available for the regional entrepreneurs. The global-pipeline model, compared to local-buzz, has a considerably higher price for maintenance. It requires trust, strategic motivation, and control over transferable information so that enterprises would be willing to engage in these information transfers. Nevertheless, once a pipeline is established, trustworthy relations begin to emerge, bringing institutionalised and customised procedures and behavioural norms (Uzzi, 1996; Bathelt, Malmberg and Maskell, 2004). The process is path-dependent and enhances the relationship between companies (local and global), pushing regions to be flexible and carefully consider their economic interests (Yeung, 2009, 2015). Because of the costly nature of pipelines, companies can afford a limited number of such links. Not all companies can permit themselves to invest in global information transfer, so it is probably related to the size and age of the firm. A correct mix of global pipelines and locally-circulating information is the best way of achieving long-term innovativeness and sustaining competitive capacity for clusters/regions. Endogenous knowledge exchange can help with the diffusion of critical knowledge, while exogenous information remains cluster-aligned with modern and global patterns and practices.

Overlapping both categories of knowledge types and diffusion models (Tab. 1), it can be expected that component information would be easily disseminated and predominate as a type of information that is exchanged within a local network or cluster. Architectural knowledge is not easily transferable; it is firm-specific and not necessarily compatible with other company's organisational processes (Tallman, Jenkins and Pinch, 2004). In the case of global pipelines, their existence is costly and goal-specific, motivating actors to sacrifice strategic/specific information in order to normalise communication (Bathelt et al., 2004). To achieve their collaborative goals, companies would be interested in making efforts and disseminate parts of architectural knowledge, in order to maintain and improve the connections between enterprises and to avoid losing already invested resources. Distant firms join efforts to overcome problematic collaboration and try to adapt and synergise with both organisational models. Thus, valuable and strategically important information is expected to represent a significant share of information circulating through global pipelines. It can ensure a pragmatic co-existence of two actors and increase the adoption rate of component knowledge. Nonetheless, such exchanges would probably be goal-specific and do not reflect architectural knowledge of the whole firm – mainly related to concrete goals.

Company-specific and path-dependent evolution of firms, embedded in architectural knowledge, contributes to the use and manipulation of knowledge, permitting some firms to react and adapt in a faster, better and less costly manner than others do. This phenomenon is called the absorptive capacity. It refers to the process of learning and adapting new knowledge, gathered from company-external sources, in order to achieve innovations (Bathelt, Malmberg and Maskell, 2004; Tallman, Jenkins and Pinch, 2004). Researchers in the relevant literature believe that the ability to operate and integrate new data into useful and innovative processes increases with each piece of new information absorbed. That is especially the case when dealing with complex knowledge of an architectural nature. In other words, absorptive capacity resembles the competence to learn, combine new data with old ways or existing knowledge in order to gain new intelligence. For the same reason and because of economic interest, companies are careful, absorbing or ignoring information based on the potential for added value while securing a part of their knowledge from reaching the buzz, ensuring temporary advantages (Bell, 2005; Bathelt, Malmberg and Maskell, 2004).

Tab. 1: Knowledge types and diffusion models

	Local Buzz	Global Pipeline
Component Knowledge	Component Knowledge has the potential to be the main object of local information flow. Most often is tacit, explicit and disaggregated information. Component data is easily accessible for other firms through spill-overs. This characteristic is ensured by automated circulation of information and costless participation. E.g. buyer-supplier relationships, resources used, workforce skills, etc.	All the information flowing through pipelines is limited and has specific characteristics required by collaboration goals. Because of strategic interests and associated expenses, mostly highly scientific and potentially innovative information is be the object of exogenous exchange. E.g. technical blueprints, production steps, R&D data, etc.
Architectural Knowledge	Is kept secret from other actors. Even if it became a part of local knowledge diffusion, usually it is very firm-specific, hard to comprehend and not accessible to stranger companies. Absorption of architectural knowledge is costly and risky, thus being inseparably linked to mother-company. It can require trust, reputational approval and more embedded inter-firm relationships to be exchanged. *Cluster-level architectural knowledge contributes and supports the existence of local buzz. E.g. internal arrangements of departments, management-employee relationships, market approach, etc.	It is probably the most important part of trans-firm, global collaboration, since it ensures comprehensible cultural and institutional contexts to accommodate the co-existence of two architectural knowledges to achieve strategic goals. Establishing a pipeline suggests that issues of trust and willingness to collaborate had been overcome, thus enhancing the ability to share architectural information. Information flowing through pipelines can be limited, omitting valuable data about historical characteristics or errors, to support positive image and continue collaboration. Expensive character of pipelines dictates that only goal-specific information is mainly to be transferred. E.g. inter-department collaboration, case-specific management decisions, network data, etc.

Source: Author's interpretation.

It is clear that information is of primary interest for policymakers to consider for a development policy. However, development can create risks for companies of falling into a trap. The innovativeness affects the openness to new knowledge – by achieving a successful outcome, enterprises are encouraged to use the same methods, information and tools, neglecting alternative and new means (Etzkowitz and Klofsten, 2005). In such cases, it is recommended to build and sustain exogenous communication channels alongside locally embedded ones, to ensure variance of sources and content (Bathelt, Malmberg and Maskell, 2004).

5. Conclusions

This paper has presented the characteristics of over- and under-socialised developmental systems, as a background and theoretical framework for innovation policy in regions. The main focus was on presenting the effects that localisation and social integration have on economic actor' capacity to create new knowledge. In the process of literature review, information, its combination and dissemination, proved to be the key concept and most important aspect on which both theories build their argumentative bodies.

Co-location and network paradigms have similar approaches, with multiple overlapping concepts, interpretations and common observations. However, their conclusions oppose each other regarding some crucial points. Cluster theory argues the importance of geographical closeness and suggests that it creates communication opportunities, lowers transactional and transportation costs, forges specialised workforce and demand, and creates space for observation and replication (Porter, 1990, 1996, 1998; Furman, Porter and Stern 2001). The basis for that are the frequent social and economic interactions achieved through continuous contacts and face-to-face meetings. Voluntary and involuntary interactions caused by close location, lead to the harmonisation of local competition and offer opportunities for co-operative market strategies. Thus, actors benefit from higher degrees of trust, exchange of valuable information and ability to monitor their neighbours, to perform a synergetic co-existence and development. In contrast, the networking argument considers innovation to be the product of communication, achieved through building ties and connections with other socially and economically embedded actors (e.g., Cooke, 1992; Granovetter, 1985; Chesbrough, 2003; West et al., 2014). The relationships affect building trust (Uzzi, 1996), enhancing communication of important data and motivating cooperation with other innovative actors, knowledge creation institutions or supportive organisations (Cepoi and Golob, 2016, 2017).

Authors of network theory do not neglect the fact that locational factors matter, acknowledging them as impacting network cohesion. Nonetheless, they argue that networks are not bounded by location, showing high added value between distant actors (Modic and Rončević, 2018).

Both theories are not completely different. For example, some authors think that a cluster can be seen as a geographically proximate network (Rocha and Sternberg, 2005) or that the network paradigm is capable of explaining clusters' innovative successes (Asheim and Coenen, 2005). However, their impact and importance vary significantly, especially for policy formulation. Considering the complex construction of innovative systems and clusters, each creates unique economic equilibria that should be considered when choosing between one or another.

Regardless of which theory to support, the most important factor is to ensure the diffusion and exchange of information for a successful innovation policy. In this regard, each theory is applicable to different circumstances. In regions where the degree of specialisation is very high and local information has a bigger impact on the developmental processes, it would be advisable to choose a cluster model and ensure the flow of local buzz. In contrast, when the region is engaged and easily interacts with various international production chains, following RIS, OI and Social Fields theories seems more beneficial. Connecting economic actors between themselves and with educational and knowledge creation institutions can mobilise their resources and achieve innovative performance. Nonetheless, the optimal combination of architectural and component data, as well as diverse knowledge-exchange sources (both regional and external) seems a mandatory factor for a cluster or a network to innovate.

References

Asheim, B. T., and Coenen, L. (2005) Knowledge bases and regional innovation systems: Comparing Nordic clusters. *Research Policy, 34*(8): 1173–1190. https://doi.org/10.1016/j.respol.2005.03.013

Baptista, R. (2001) Geographical clusters and innovation Diffusion. *Technological Forecasting and Social Change, 66*(1): 31–46. https://doi.org/10.1016/S0040-1625(99)00057-8

Bathelt, H., Malmberg, A., and Maskell, P. (2004) Clusters and knowledge: Local buzz, global pipelines and the process of knowledge creation. *Progress in Human Geography, 28*(1): 31–56. https://doi.org/10.1191/0309132504ph469oa

Beckert, J. (2010) How do fields change? the interrelations of institutions, networks, and cognition in the dynamics of markets. *Organization Studies*, *31*(5): 605–627. https://doi.org/10.1177/0170840610372184

Bell, G. G. (2005) Research notes and comments, clusters, networks and firm innovativeness. *Strategy Management Journal*, *26*: 287–295

Besednjak Valic, T. (2019) Innovation, digitalisation, and the HPC in the Danube Region. In: Roncevic, B., Coscodaru, R. and Fric, U. (eds.), *Go with the Flow: High Performance Computing and Innovations in the Danube Region*. London, Budapest, Ljubljana: Vega Press Ltd., 22–46.

Besednjak Valič, T., Kolar, J., and Lamut, U. (2020) Three scenarios of innovation and technology transfer: The case of key enabling technologies in the Danube Region. *Journal of Engineering and Applied Sciences*, *15*: 3619–3623.

Brenner, T., Cantner, U., Fornahl, D., Fromhold-Eisebith, M., and Werker, C. (2011) Regional innovation systems, clusters, and knowledge networking. *Papers in Regional Science*, *90*(2): 243–249. https://doi.org/10.1111/j.1435-5957.2011.00368.x

Capello, R. (2011) Location, regional growth and local development theories. *Aestimum*, *58*: 1–25. https://doi.org/10.13128/Aestimum-9559

Cepoi, V. (2016) Do social forces matter? A model for innovation and development performance. *Research in Social Change*, *8*(3): 4–27.

Cepoi, V. (2017) Innovation performance in the EU comparative perspective. *Comparative Sociology*, *16*(4): 555–579. https://doi.org/10.1163/15691330-12341433

Cepoi, V. (2019) Interplay of social forces: A focus on regional innovation processes. *The social sciences 14*(12): 423–430.

Cepoi, V. (2020) A meta-analysis and explanation of innovation processes through the outline of social fields theory. *Research in Social Change*, 12(3): 15–31. DOI:10.2478/rsc-2020-0012.

Cepoi, V., and Golob, T. (2016) Regional innovation performance: Measuring development in cultural, social and economic perspectives. *Innovative Issues and Approaches in Social Sciences*, *9*(1): 242–260. https://doi.org/10.12959/issn.1855-0541.iiass-2016-no1-art13

Chesbrough, H. W. (2003) The era of open innovation. *MIT Sloan Management Review*, *44*(3): 34–42.

Cooke, P. (1992) Regional innovation systems: Competitive regulation in the new Europe. *Geoforum*, *23*(3): 365–382. https://doi.org/10.1016/0016-7185(92)90048-9

Cooke, P. (2001) Regional innovation systems, clusters, and the knowledge economy. *Industrial and Corporate Change, 10*(4): 945–974. https://doi.org/10.1093/icc/10.4.945

Doloreux, D. and Parto, S. (2005) Regional innovation systems: Current discourse and unresolved issues. *Technology in Society, 27*(2): 133–153. https://doi.org/10.1016/j.techsoc.2005.01.002

Džajić Uršič, E. and Rončević, B. (2017) Industrial symbiotic networks in the information society: Research challenges and perspectives. In: Rončević, B. and Tomšič, M. (eds.), *Information Society and Its Manifestations: Economy, Politics, Culture*. Frankfurt am Main: Peter Lang, 71–81.

Erman, N. (2020) Prospects for innovation performance on European level. *Research in Social Change, 12*(3): 100–114. DOI:10.2478/rsc-2020-0016

Etzkowitz, H., and Klofsten, M. (2005) The innovating region: Toward a theory of knowledge-based regional development. *R and D Management, 35*(3): 243–255. https://doi.org/10.1111/j.1467-9310.2005.00387.x

European Commission, (2010) *Communication from the Commission to the European Council Europe 2020 A European strategy for smart, sustainable and inclusive growth,* https://ec.europa.eu/transparency/regdoc/rep/1/2010/EN/COM-2010-2020-1-EN-MAIN-PART-1.PDF

European Commission, (2019) *Reflection Paper towards a Sustainable Europe by 2030.* https://ec.europa.eu/commission/sites/beta-political/files/rp_sustainable_europe_30-01_en_web.pdf

Feser, E. J., and Bergman, E. M. (2000) National industry cluster templates: A framework for applied regional cluster analysis. *Regional Studies, 34*(1): 1–19. https://doi.org/10.1080/00343400050005844

Fligstein, N. (2001) Social skill and the theory of fields. *Sociological Theory, 19*(2): 105–125.

Fric, U. and Roncevic, B. (2018) E-simbioza: Leading a way to a Circular Economy through Industrial Symbiosis in Slovenia. *Socijalna ekologija: časopis za ekološku misao i sociologijska istraživanja okoline, 27*(2): 119–140.

Fric, U. and Rončević, B. (2020) Towards transdisciplinary research on industrial symbiosis networks. *Journal of Engineering and Applied Sciences, 15*(17): 3168–3177.

Fric, U., Rončević, B., and Džajić, Uršič, E. (2020) Role of computer software tools in industrial symbiotic networks and the examination of sociocultural factors. *Environmental progress & sustainable energy, 39*(2): e13364.

Furman, J. L., Porter, M. E., and Stern, S. (2001) The determinants of national innovative capacity. *Research Policy,* 31(6): 899-933.

Gangaliuc, C. (2019) The measurement of innovation for management, research and policy. *Research in Social Change, 11*(2): 35–57. DOI:10.2478/rsc-2019-0008.

Giuliani, E., Pietrobelli, C., and Rabellotti, R. (2005) Upgrading in global value chains: Lessons from Latin American clusters. *World Development,* 33(4): 549–573. https://doi.org/10.1016/j.worlddev.2005.01.002

Golob, T. (2014) Exploring identifications in the transnational social sphere: The potential of social fields. *Sociologija i prostor: časopis za istraživanje prostornog i sociokulturnog razvoja*, *52*(2): 123–140.

Golob, T. and Makarovič, M. (2017) Self-organisation and development: A comparative approach to post-communist transformations from the perspective of social systems theory. *Europe-Asia studies, 69*(10): 1499–1525.

Golob, T. and Makarovič, M. (2018) Student mobility and transnational social ties as factors of reflexivity. *Social Sciences,* 7(3): 1–18.

Grabher, G. (2006) Trading routes, bypasses, and risky intersections: Mapping the travels of "networks" between economic sociology and economic geography. *Progress in Human Geography, 30*(2): 163–189. https://doi.org/10.1191/0309132506ph600oa

Granovetter, M. (1985) Economic action and social structure: The problem of embeddedness. *The Sociology of Economic Life*, *91*(3): 481–510.

Hafner, A. and Modic, D. (2020) European automotive technological innovation systems in the age of disruption: the suppliers' view. *Research in Social Change*, 12(3): 53–77, DOI:10.2478/rsc-2020-0014.

Hess, M., and Yeung, H. W.-C. (2006) Whither global production networks in economic geography? Past, present, and future. *Environment and Planning A*, *38*(7): 1193–1204. https://doi.org/10.1068/a38463

Insead, I. G., Moskison, R. E., Beal, B. D., Wan, W. P. (2005) Explaining the clustering of international expansion moves: A critical test in the us telecommunication industry. *Academy of Management Journal*, *48*(2): 297–319

Kleindienst, P. (2017) Understanding the different dimensions of human dignity: Analysis of the decision of the Constitutional Court of the Republic of Slovenia on the "Tito Street" Case. *DANUBE: Law and Economics Review, 8*(3): 117–137, doi: 10.1515/danb-2017-0009.

Kleindienst, P. (2019) Zgodovinski temelji sodobne paradigme človekovega dostojanstva. *Phainomena* 28(108–109) 259–282, doi: 10.32022/PHI28.2019.108-109.11.

Kleindienst, P. and Matevž, T. (2017) Human dignity as the foundation of democratic political culture: Legal and philosophical perspective. *Law, Culture and the Humanities, 1*(20), doi: 10.177/143872117738229.

Kleindienst, P. and Matevž, T. (2018) Človekovo dostojanstvo kot del politične kulture v novih demokracijah: postkomunistična Slovenija. *Bogoslovni vestnik, 78* (1): 159–172, UDK: 316.334.3(497.4).

Lazzarini, S. G., Miller, G. J. and Zenger, T. R. (2008) Dealing with the paradox of embeddedness: The role of contracts and trust in facilitating movement out of committed relationships. *Organization Science, 19*(5): 709–728. https://doi.org/10.1287/orsc.1070.0336

Makarovič, M., Šušteršič, J. and Rončević, B (2014) Is Europe 2020 set to fail?: The cultural political economy of the EU grand strategies. *European Planning Studies*, 22(3): 610–626.

Mileva Boshkoska, B., Rončević, B. and Džajić Uršič, E. (2018) Modeling and evaluation of the possibilities of forming a regional industrial symbiosis networks. *Social Sciences, 7*(1), 13; doi.org/10.3390/socsci7010013

Modic, D. and Roncevic, B. (2018) Social topography for sustainable innovation policy: Putting institutions, social networks and cognitive frames in their place. *Comparative Sociology*. https://doi.org/10.1163/15691330-12341452

Pandiloska Jurak, A. (2020) Public policy instrument evaluation in service of enabling grand strategy discourse – Case of horizon 2020 key indicators. *Research in Social Change 11*(2): 97–121.

Pandiloska Jurak, A. and Pinterič, U. (2012) Assessment of municipalities' performances in Slovenia. *Transylvanian review of administrative sciences*, (35): 121–137.

Parto, S. (2008) Innovation and economic activity: An institutional analysis of the role of clusters in industrializing economies. *Journal of Economic Issues, 42*(4): 1005–1030. https://doi.org/10.1080/00213624.2008.11507200.

Porter, M. (1990) Competitive advantage of nations. *Competitive Intelligence Review, 1*(1): 14–14. https://doi.org/10.1002/cir.3880010112

Porter, M. E. (1996) Competitive advantage, agglomeration economies, and regional policy. *International Regional Science Review, 19*(1&2), 85–94.

Porter, M. E. (1998) Clusters and the new economics of competition. *Harvard Business Review*, 76(6): 77–90.

Pratt, A. C. (2004) Creative clusters: Towards the governance of the creative industries production system? *Media International Australia*, 112(1): 50–66.

Rocha, H. O. (2004) Entrepreneurship and development: The role of clusters. *Small Business Economics, 23*(5): 363–400. https://doi.org/10.1007/s11187-015-9643-3

Rocha, H. O. and Sternberg, R. (2005) Entrepreneurship: The role of clusters theoretical perspectives and empirical evidence from Germany. *Small Business Economics*, 24(3): 267–292. https://doi.org/10.1007/s11187-005-1993-9

Romanelli, E. & Khessina, O. M. (2005) Regional industrial identity: Cluster configurations and economic development. *Organization Science*, *16*(4): 344–358. https://doi.org/10.1287/orsc.1050.0131

Rončević, B. (2019) Cultural political economy of Europe 2020: Jean Monnet chair CPE 2020 and its impact. *Research in Social Change*, 11(2): 5–13. DOI:10.2478/rsc-2019-0006

Roncevic, B. and Besednjak Valic, T. (2019) How to think about regional development agencies as a sociologist. *The Social Sciences,* 14(9): 326–334 https://doi.org/10.36478/sscience.2019.326.334

Rončević, B. and Fric, U. (2015) Researching industrial symbiosis: Challenges and dilemmas. In: Povh, Janez (ed.), *Applied Modelling and Computing in Social Science*. Frankfurt am Main: Peter Lang, 35–49.

Rončević, B. and Fric, U. (2017) Path-creation in the information society. In: Rončević, B. and Tomšič, M. (eds.), *Information Society and Its Manifestations: Economy, Politics, Culture*. Frankfurt am Main: Peter Lang, 41–53.

Rončević, B. and Makarovič, M. (2010) Towards the strategies of modern societies: Systems and social processes. *Innovation: The European Journal of Social Science Research*, *23*(3): 223–239.

Rončević, B. and Makarovič, M. (2011) Societal steering in theoretical perspective: Social becoming as an analytical solution. *Polish Sociological Review, 176*(4): 461–472.

Rončević, Borut, Šušteršič, J., Wostner, P., and Besednjak Valič, T. (2010) Quo Vadis, Slovenia? Between framework conditions and internal capabilities. *Managing Global Transitions*, *8*(4): 353–380.

Rončević, B. and Tomšič, M. (2017) Perspectives of information society: Bricolage of manifestations. In: Rončević, B. and Tomšič, M. (eds.), *Information Society and Its Manifestations: Economy, Politics, Culture*. Frankfurt am Main: Peter Lang, 9–21.

Rosemberg, N, (2004) Innovation and Economic Growth, *OECD paper.*

Schoales, J. (2006) Alpha clusters: Creative innovation in local economies. *Economic Development Quarterly*, *20*(2): 162–177. https://doi.org/10.1177/0891242405285932

Sohn, D. W., and Kenney, M. (2007). Universities, clusters, and innovation systems: The case of Seoul, Korea. *World Development*, *35*(6): 991–1004. doi.org/10.1016/j.worlddev.2006.05.008.

Tallman, S., Jenkins, M., and Pinch, S. (2004) Knowledge, clusters, and competitive advantage. *The Academy of Management Review*, *29*(2): 258–271.

Uyarra, E. (2009) What is evolutionary about "regional systems of innovation"? Implications for regional policy. *Journal of Evolutionary Economics*, 20(1): 115–137. https://doi.org/10.1007/s00191-009-0135-y

Uzzi, B. (1996) The sources and consequences of embeddedness for the economic performance of organizations: The network effect. *American Sociological Review*, *61*(4). https://doi.org/10.2307/2096399

West, J., Salter, A., Vanhaverbeke, W., and Chesbrough, H. (2014) Open innovation: The next decade. *Research Policy*, *43*(5): 805–811. https://doi.org/10.1016/j.respol.2014.03.001

Wicks, A. C., Berman, S. L., and Jones, T. M. (1999) The structure of optimal trust: Moral and strategic implications. *Academy of Management Review*, *24*(1): 99–116. https://doi.org/10.5465/AMR.1999.1580443

Yeung, H. W. (2009) Production networks, and urban and regional development: A geographer's perspective on multinational enterprises and the global economy. *Growth and Change*, *40*(2): 197–226.

Yeung, H. W. Chung. (2015) Regional development in the global economy: A dynamic perspective of strategic coupling in global production networks. *Regional Science Policy and Practice*, *7*(1): 1–23. https://doi.org/10.1111/rsp3.12055

Innovation 2.0 for Smart, Inclusive and Sustainable Growth in Regional Context

Tamara Besednjak Valič

Open Innovation and Its Impacts on Interorganisational Stability: A SOFIA Perspective Addressing the Sustainable Growth in Regional Context

Abstract: We live in times of constant adaptation to changes. Business sectors and research sectors are characterised by constant processes of innovation. Innovation *per se* brings changes to both knowledge databases and to organisations. The latter need to properly manage the upcoming change arising from innovation. In the paradigm of Open Innovation, the management of change in companies is crucial to maintain the network of actors and properly manage the day-to-day business and respond to market demands. How should firms behave in such a position of constant flux to assure sustainable growth in regional context? We attempt to establish a model based on SOFIA illuminating the interplay of social forces that contribute to the stable progress and functional operation and successful implementation of developed innovation.

Keywords: Open innovation, sustainable growth, regional development, changes, change management, social fields, social theory, SOFIA

1. Introduction

We live in times of constant adaptation to changes. Business and research sectors are characterised by constant processes of innovation. Innovation can bring changes to both knowledge databases and to organisations. The latter need to properly manage the upcoming change arising from the innovation. In the paradigm of Open Innovation, the management of change in companies is crucial to be able to maintain the network of actors and to properly manage the day-to-day business and respond to market demands. The question of Open Innovation and its impacts on inter-organisational stability and social fields are subjected to vast interest of different fields of research – from sociology, economy to psychology – and are the topic of regional innovation systems remains a focal point for sociologists (Cepoi, 2019; Modic and Rončević, 2018; Cepoi and Golob, 2017; Cepoi and Golob, 2016; Rončević and Modic, 2012; Rončević and Besednjak Valič, 2019; Besednjak Valič et al. 2020; Rončević et al. 2010; Rončević et al., 2018).

The present article enters the arena of Open Innovation, focusing on the organisational aspect of firms and combines the view with a holistic sociological approach of explaining Regional Innovation Systems through the prism of Social Fields theory. Doing so, the following research questions were prepared to guide the line of thought:

First: How should firms behave in such a position of constant flux to assure sustainable growth in regional context?
Second: Does the answer lie in the suggestion on selecting and implementing proper organisational structure?
Third: Consequently, what is the interplay of social forces inside and outside the organisation?

The article is structured as follows: firstly, the global trends are discussed in consideration with the role of innovation, megatrends are presented outlining their impact on different life aspects. Secondly, the paradigm of Open Innovation is introduced, encompassing main impacts to organisations and their position within the flux of global trends. In line with Open Innovation thinking, the position of organisations is reviewed from the perspective of the knowledge economy and intellectual capital. Further, how organisations can manage the change from Closed to Open Innovation is discussed. The article continues the line of thought focusing on the role of institutions in sustainable growth and regional development and finishes with the introduction of a tentative conceptual model of social forces influencing the success of the Open Innovation paradigm.

2. Innovation and Change in a Flux of Global Trends

'The only constant in life is change', stated Ancient Greek philosopher Heraclitus. In today's interconnected world, the change is desired to be driven since the situation otherwise seems to be 'out of control' (Rončević and Modic, 2012, p.313) and the world is continuously restructuring in the never-ending process of 'social becoming' (Rončević and Makarovič, 2011, 2010). The EU, for example, reduces the risks with major investments in research and innovation through mechanisms such as H2020 (see more in Pandiloska Jurak, 2019). All changes and innovations have to be in line with the main values and principles on which the EU is based (Kleindienst, 2017; Kleindienst and Tomšič, 2017; Kleindienst and Tomšič, 2018). However, this situation is not new, and sociology, alongside other disciplines, aims to understand and interpret the global trends that have shaped social change ever since the industrial revolution (ibid.). The recent global events, the COVID-19 pandemics, and the threat of global economic crisis have contributed to understanding and mutual agreement that innovation is a key tool to manage and control global trends. The global trends, therefore, are understood as omnipresent forces that stem from the past, shape the present and will have an impact on the future (Singh et al., 2009). It is no wonder that organisations monitor and seek insights so they can be prepared for how to operate in the future. Organisations invest in management tools and develop scenarios of driving, adapting, or at least coping with the future trends (ibid). Various models and standards based on specific criteria and methodological tools measure and value the quality, effectiveness, efficiency and excellence (see Pandiloska Jurak and Pinterič, 2012). Coping is understood as seeking business opportunities to assure one's position in the market and to sustain operations. Research shows (Becker and Freeman, 2006) that constant adjustment of portfolios to be in line with global trends contribute to growth in profits.

Different authors write about different global trends but most appropriate for this discussion seems to be the elaboration provided by Singh et al. (2009) that establishes a triangle of global trends, inevitably interrelated. These are Globalisation, Open Innovation, and the Rise of Networks. All three are constituted around Global Consumer Trends. Each of the outlined trends consists of sub-trends as follows in the table below:

A careful examination of the above table shows that all the three megatrends are inevitably interrelated with knowledge. It is knowledge-based economic activities that underpin the majority of processes of globalisation. Knowledge is an asset that cannot be stored away; instead, it increases in value upon interaction and trial-and-error processes (Mattes, 2010). The global trends of the past and today have contributed to our society becoming knowledge-based. Knowledge is being turned into an economic resource, its embodiment becoming an indispensable asset for economic survival and change (ibid, p.1). The process of obtaining knowledge (i.e., learning) has inevitably become the most important process in the 'knowledge-intensive economy' (Lundvall and Johnson, 2016). It is the process of learning, providing engaged persons access to new knowledge; it is also the reflection of new knowledge, which can lead to innovation and new discoveries (Mattes, 2010). This is why innovation underpins all the above-mentioned global trends.

The topic of innovation has long been present in organisational literature, with authors defining it in a very similar manner. Barnett (1953) defines it as inventing something new, while Carroll (1967) and Becker and Whistler (1967) understand innovation as a social process of adoption rather than one of

Tab. 1: Megatrends with corresponding sub-trends (adapted from Singh et al., 2009)

Megatrend	Sub-trend	Short description
Globalisation	Cultural multipolarity	The ability to establish culture and manage it through coordination and dissemination.
	Cultural Flow	Means the exchange and fusion of cultures through internet media and the web.
	Global Workforce	The global workforce is more mobile because of emerging technologies and economic integration. Workforce faces competition on global basis.
	Emergence of BRIC[a]	The BRIC countries are expected to take over the G6 in terms of GDP by 2047
	Social responsibility	Due to globalisation, the world is more focused towards sustainable development
	Democracy and Emphasis of Individual Rights	Interrelated to the improvement of individual position in society, connected to societal development and more equality
	Global Counter-Terrorism	Terrorism is connected with a lack of democracy and of individual rights.
Rise of Networks	Proliferation of information technologies	Due to this, the value chain of many industries is being changed.
	Connectivity	Internet-related technologies redefined the ways people connect and interact
	Convergence	Refers to the amalgamation of previously separated technologies of audio, video, Internet and data. These technologies now interact with one another.
	GRID Computing	Provides scientists the processing power of thousands of worldwide connected computers, to enable them to deal with huge amounts of data
	Ubiquitous Computing	Involves intelligent microprocessors in everyday objects connected with each other via the internet
Open Innovation	Crossing disciplines and boundaries	Quest for innovations merges the disciplines like biotechnology, IT, nanotechnology, medical science, business science and others.
	Custumers as co-producers	Information technologies enable companies to collect and analyse customers' feedback.

Tab. 1: Continued

Megatrend	Sub-trend	Short description
Global Consumer Trends	Cultural Identity Exploration	Consumers face unimaginable cultural flows; this is complemented with consumerism adapted to nationalistic and religious values.
	Individualisation	Consumers around the world expectations regarding the product they demand are more precise. Consumer can customise music, media and even advertising through technology.
	Premiumisation	Characterised by the democratisation of luxury as more consumers are able to afford luxury.
	Gender Complexity	Blurring of traditional gender roles since women are part of global workforce and men are taking part in household chores
	Appearance of Three-nagers	People in their thirties desire the look of teenagers.
	Eco-iconism	Follows the trend for eco-friendly products – is a sub trend of Social responsibility.
	Offer Transistency	Products and services becoming transient – for one time use only.
	Hiving	Generation X is noted to embrace the lifestyle of the homebody. More money is spent on renovating and decorating a home to become a cosy place for gatherings

a BRIC stands for Brazil, Russia, India, and China

discovery. Mansfeld (1963) makes a distinction between innovation and imitation: innovation is when an organisation uses, for the first time, a new product, service, process or idea. When the same innovation is used by other social systems, this is imitation. Knight introduces the notion of a relevant environment that is subjected to the impact of innovation (1967). Innovation is understood as change that is new to an organisation (ibid.). To summarise, the different definitions connect innovation with the following aspects (Pierce and Delbecq, 1977): (1) first use of an idea with subsequent use being understood as imitation; (2) the first use of an idea, product or service in organisations with similar goals; and (3) the first use by the focal organisation. At this point, it seems useful to understand innovation as generation, acceptance and implementation of new processes, products or services for the first time within an organisation (ibid.). Additionally, innovation occurs on various levels and very often requires different conditions (Gangaliuc, 2019).

Much work was done to understand how the National and Regional Innovation System works to keep up with the global trends. Knowledge, obtained primarily through formal education and informal education, is an important tool and driver of innovation.

3. On Open Innovation

Ever since the publishing of 'Open Innovation: researching a new paradigm' edited by Chesbrough (2006), much has been said and written about Open Innovation. The topic steadily became the most written-about topic in innovation management (Huizingh, 2011). A quick Google Scholar search of the term provides nearly four million hits,[1] and the works of Chesbrough on the topic have gained more than 40,000 citations[2] (Google Scholar, July 2020). The topic is being discussed in a vast variety of fields, including economics, psychology and sociology. However, why has the concept gained so much interest from the research community(ies)? Following the definition, the concept embraces the essence of the innovation process. Chesbrough et al. (2006) define Open Innovation as the use of purposive inflows and outflows of knowledge, to accelerate internal innovation, and to expand the markets for external use of innovation.

However, as Chesbrough writes (2012), there are two major ways of understanding and defining Open Innovation. Apart from this, the second is the one developed by von Hippel (2005), which is based and builds on the concept of open-source software. The essence of the second theory is that all innovation is free for everyone to use and apply. In this view, IP protection and business models have no role to play. This definition does not deal with the question of how an organisation should earn a return and fund research that results in innovation. In contrast, Chesbrough's (ibid.) definition of Open Innovation is concerned with business models a firm uses and whether they can use to successfully embrace the openness of their boundaries. One of the mechanisms is most definitely IP protection. Innovations protected by IP are able to be 'commercialized by the company, business models are created, and capital investments are required to create growth. The real social impact of an

1 Ten years ago the term provided over two million hits (Huizingh, 2011).
2 The reported number of citations in 2010 was around 2,000 citations.

innovation only arrives after it is commercialized' (Chesbrough, 2012, p. 22). The main dynamics Chesbrough is interested in is the one embracing the view of the organisation as the main generator of innovations and the organisations' concern regarding how to commercialise the innovation in order to assure financial success to fund further development and growth. Such orientation is the core essence of every organisation that has the aim and desire to remain operative and to continue to assure social impact.

Chesbrough (2012) also visually explains the dynamic relationship between market, market creation, and organisations operating in such conditions. With a strong technological base, both internal and external, the organisation can develop their research activities with internal and external partners to assure position at primary market, via spin-off companies the new markets are created and with engaging in out-licensing, the organisation assures a share in other organisations' markets. There are three stages of the Open Innovation process: (1) research, (2) development, and (3) commercialisation (Bujor and Avasilcai, 2018). For each of the initial ideas there are three mentioned stages before the invention (if research is successful, if development is possible and if product is commercialised) reaches the market.

Another important aspect in Chesbrough's definition of Open Innovation is the two-fold nature of its relationship towards innovation generation. As Bujor and Avasilcai (2018) observed, the flow of innovation is (a) outside in, and (b) inside out. The outside in view focuses on processes of opening up to external sources of knowledge and information in order to increase research and innovation efficiency, where the second view allows the company to release the unused and underutilised ideas to other businesses for them to use them better. The latter view has received less attention from the researchers and practitioners (ibid, 2018) and, therefore, remains less explored than the first view.

Open Innovation is set up in contrast to closed innovation characterised by innovation occurring only inside companies. Organisations develop innovation ideas and then develop, build, market, distribute and finance them by themselves (Huizingh, 2011). However, a fully closed innovation process is difficult for companies to maintain; therefore, only a few companies manage to do so; most engage in a somewhat half-closed innovation. Specifically, every organisation is dependent on outside economic, political and cultural settings, and changes occurring therein. As discussed above, globalisation and market conditions, and new technologies are some of the most important trends influencing the positions of organisations.

4. Knowledge Economy and Intellectual Capital for Open Innovation

Following the demands of the global trends, the companies enter the era of the knowledge economy (Barney, 1991; Drucker, 1985; Grant, 1991) or even 'knowledge intensive economy' (Lundvall and Johnson, 2016), following the demand to nurture and foster highest levels of intellectual capital, which is seen as the most valuable resource of the companies (Amri et al., 2010; Ramezan, 2011; Hafner and Modic, 2020). Ramezan (2011) writes on three inevitable parameters of the intellectual capital of an organisation: (1) human capital, (2) structural capital, and (3) relational capital. All three seem to overlap heavily with the three dimensions of the social field organised within an organisation. More on Social Fields is developed in the next chapters. As operationalised by Chen et al. (2004), each of the parameters of intellectual capital can be measured as follows:

(a) human capital is measured by competence, attitude and creativity of the employee;
(b) structural capital is measured by corporate culture, organisational structure, organisational learning, operation process, and information system;
(c) relational capital or customer capital is measured by basic marketing capability, market intensity, customer loyalty.

The latter, however, requires the specific notion that relational capital describes the special value of relationships that the firm establishes and maintains with actors external to it (Martín de Castro and López Sáez, 2008, p. 26). Here we refer to one of the basic prerequisites of Open Innovation to reach beyond our boundaries to foster innovation. Regardless, in the context of entering the knowledge era and Open Innovation paradigm, Ramezan (2011) concludes that organisations will have to change to be more adaptable and flexible to enhance their intellectual capital. This is the only way for them to keep up with the innovation leaders and capture opportunities in the dynamic environment shaped by global trends.

5. Managing the Change from Closed to Open Innovation – Interorganisational Aspect

Introducing innovation, especially incremental innovation, has become a prerogative for a firm to survive. In recent years, firms have started to reach out in their search for knowledge, seeking it outside their organisational boundaries.

In this respect, organisations needed to undergo the change from the Closed Innovation paradigm to the Open Innovation paradigm.

To be part of Open Innovation, organisations had to adjust their management tools and strategies to facilitate the transition towards Open Innovation. This transition is an incremental change for the company; some authors (Chiaroni et al., 2011) apply different models of change that companies can utilise while transitioning to new. A useful one is Lewin's model of organisational change with three stages of unfreezing, moving and refreezing (institutionalising) but within this, Chiaroni et al.'s (2011) proposed four dimensions seem more tangible. They outline four dimensions managers need to monitor and use to upscale the organisation to Open Innovation: networks, organisational structures, evaluation processes, and knowledge management systems (ibid).

On the path towards the adoption of Open Innovation, companies inevitably go through the three stages of change, as according to Kurt Lewin (Cummings et al., 2016). While on this path, companies must increase the absorptive capacity of the organisation (Vanhaverbeke et al., 2008; Robertson et al., 2012) and several authors write extensively over the topic (Zobel, 2016; Naqshbandi and Tabche, 2018; Xia and Roper, 2016).

The second important factor to successfully transit to Open Innovation is the relationship with external stakeholders, namely the network. These relationships can be twofold: either explorative or exploitative (Xia and Roper, 2016); in their empirical study, the authors confirmed the explorative relationships are lubricated by R&D, and the exploitative networks are more connected to absorptive capacity. Additionally, there is a question of whether it should be the organisations alone in the process of establishing the partnerships. Some authors (Lee et al., 2010; Spithoven, 2010) suggest it is intermediary organisations' role to help build networks and build trust among organisations. The intermediary organisations can be research centres or regional development agencies (Rončević and Valič, 2018), trade unions or regulating agencies, and even advocacy groups (Beckert, 2010).

Having said all that, we keep in mind the above-mentioned four organisational dimensions that need to be properly addressed to successfully transit from Closed to Open Innovation (Chiaroni et al., 2010). The networks are important since Open Innovation requires the innovating firm to nurture an extensive network of collaborators. Doing so, the organisation must establish numerous relationships with various partners, in particular universities and research institutions (Perkmann and Walsh, 2007; Lundvall and Jensen, 2016; Majetić et al., 2020; Džajić Uršič, 2020). The nature of such relationships can be explorative or exploitative (March, 1991), and every organisation operating within a paradigm of Open Innovation must be able to manage both types of relationships within their network organisations. To be able to maintain all different types of networks and relationships but also to be able to operate properly in a new paradigm, every organisation must set specific organisational structures in place. This refers to internal networks, complementary to external ones, that are devoted to access, integrate and process 'acquired knowledge into the firm's innovation processes' (Chiaroni, 2011, p. 36). The ability to learn is vital, and firms must institutionalise learning processes (Lundvall and Jensen, 2016; Ljubotina, 2020). Additionally, organisational structures must establish supporting roles[3] for Open Innovation implementation and establish a reward system that will support the transition to Open Innovation (Chiaroni, 2011).

The third tool that must be set in place is evaluation. It occurs on several levels internally, and external environments must be evaluated and constantly monitored for potential new technologies or new forms of involvement of external sources (Chiaroni, 2011).

Finally, the fourth tool is an established knowledge management system; the most usual ones are a combination of ICT and adoption of intellectual property management systems (ibid.). As Modic and Damij (2018, p. 93) elaborate, 'knowledge management is a functional group of tasks inside the strategic IPR management'.

The change in firms from the Closed Innovation paradigm to the Open Innovation paradigm is incremental. It is understood there are firms that are more eager to engage in the change and others who operate more cautiously and are therefore rather wait in their transition. Lundvall and Jensen (2016) distinguish between 'front' learners and 'catching-up' learners (p. 111). However, Huizingh (2010) expresses an interesting division when it comes to Open Innovation: some companies are only integrating the concept into their usual innovation management. Chesbrough and Crowther (2006) learned that early adopters of Open Innovation do not create new processes and metrics but rather tend to integrate Open Innovation paradigmatic stances into running processes.

3 Supporting roles can be either leaders who champion the decision to transit to Open Innovation or gate keepers who manage the relations with external environment (Chiaroni, 2011).

6. Role of Institutions in Sustainable Growth and Regional Development

To this point, we have been referring to the aspects of Open Innovation within the context of individual firms. However, considering the nature of open boundaries to the immediate environment and the importance of networking, we have to take a broader look to be able to assess the nature of relationships that are happening with the immediate environment of the individual organisation. As innovation and technological development do not always seem to have a positive effect on immediate economic activity in a region (e.g., losing manual jobs in exchange for technologically more demanding ones) (Malecki, 1987), innovation with assistance to technology now seems the principal source of development for regions[4] and nations (Valič, 2019; also Pandiloska Jurak, 2020; Cepoi, 2019). In this context, the benefits of the Open Innovation paradigm are advocated as a generator of further development not only for firms but also for Regional Innovation System,[5] which are therefore inevitably dependent on geographical scale and knowledge created within their boundaries (Asheim et al., 2016; Lundvall and Jensen, 2016; Doloreux and Parto, 2005; Cooke et al., 1997) and operate as their own social fields (Modic and Rončević, 2018). Despite the changes in technological development globalisation had on working remotely, and despite the rise of the global workforce, the regional networks, in geographical context still play an important role in knowledge flows between organisations (see also Simard and West, 2006). Governments, in desire to strengthen the existing knowledge flows, propose investing efforts to strengthen them, contributing to strengthening the regional systems of innovation. RIS are also understood as entities that can influence regional change, especially in their ability to contribute to Path Development (Isaken and Trippl, 2016). Apart from that, it is argued that regional competitive advantage can

---

4 The concept of 'region' in the context of present article refers to a unit of space, usually smaller than the national economy. In this context, a region can be an administrative unit, or a unit characterised by geographical boundaries or cultural boundaries, always within national context. It is usually structured around a dominant city around, its historical concentration of some resource (or factor of production) consequently evolved into specialisation in a certain type of industry (e.g. wood) or type of activity (e.g. R&D) (Malecki, 1987).

5 Regional Innovation System is understood as Cooke et al. (1997) and Asheim et al. (2016) understood and continue to elaborate it. In the context of present article, we will use the term 'Regional Innovation System' for a geographical unit that captures the knowledge transfer, supporting the innovation processes.

be acquired by firm-specific competences obtained through learning processes operating on a regional basis (Doloreux and Parto, 2005). The skills and knowledge derive from the 'localised capabilities'[6] (p. 134). Localised capabilities, therefore, have to exist in order for development and competitiveness to occur. The capabilities in such cases include institutional endowment, structures, knowledge and skills (ibid.) and legislation (Kleindienst, 2019). In such an environment, some write of the 'networkisation of society' (Rončević and Tomšič, 2017), meaning networking as prerogative for Open Innovation to occur.

In the paradigm of Open Innovation, in which the interplay of organisations is crucial, governments can do much to contribute to facilitate and increase inter-organisational networking. In Montenegro, for example, it is the policymakers who expect organisations to take the lead (Gangaliuc and Fric, 2019; Pezzini, 2007), emphasising the importance of multi-level governance resulting from the processes of decentralisation. Actors in such an approach are not in a command/control relationship but rather co-operate vertically or horizontally. Cities and regions are partners and different levels of government are in charge for the implementation of joint projects (pp. 24–25).

7. Social Forces Influencing the Success of the Open Innovation Paradigm – A Tentative Theoretical Model Based on SOFIA

Much has been written on Regional Innovation Systems, but in recent years the topic has become more present also in sociological theory. In particular, authors such as Rončević and Modic (Rončević, 2011, 2020; Roncevic and Modic, 2011, 2012, 2018; Rončević and Besednjak, 2019) but also Golob and Cepoi (2017), contributed vastly towards the understanding of Regional Innovation Systems as social fields, in which three main social forces influence one another contributing towards shape and development of the field. Their work contributed to the development of SOFIA. The three social forces are (1) institutions, (2) networks, and (3) cognitive frames and are in line with the proposition if Beckert (2010). Different authors have researched how each of the three social forces structure innovation (Modic and Rončević, 2018). With SOFIA, we are closer to understanding how Regional Innovation Systems are shaped and how they change: they are dynamic systems with open boundaries, in which global trends inevitably impact all actors operating within such systems. The

6 Localised capabilities, according to Doloreux and Parto (2005) are specialised resources, skills, and institutions and share of common social and cultural values.

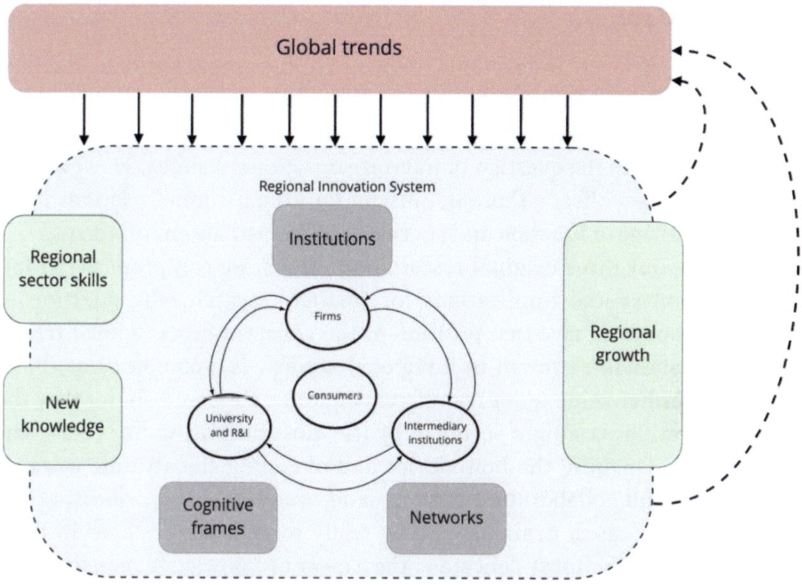

Picture 1: Dynamics and interplay of social forces in the Regional Innovation System
Source: Own work

important notion about Regional Innovation Systems is also that knowledge, apart from being determined geographically, is also determined by cultural, social and political aspects.

Institutions are the force that contributes to shaping the social field by providing legal structures (Fligstein and McAdam, 2012). Networks are an essential part of every social field, in which individuals and organisations can position themselves within the social space and establish stronger or weaker ties among each other and outside the field. In a system of Open Innovation, vast networks of relations are prerogative for functioning. Lastly, cognitive frames can be understood as a mental toolkit for individuals to be able to interpret knowledge to manifest skills and contribute towards the implementation of relevant developmental strategies. Cognitive frames provide the 'mental organization of the social environment' (Beckert, 2010, p. 610).

8. Conclusions

The question of Open Innovations, impacts to inter-organisational stability, and the social field of Regional Innovation Systems remain an interesting topic. Not much research done under the broader topic of Regional Innovation systems has dealt with the question of inter-organisational stability. However, the present discussion offers a thorough insight into the nature of relationships a firm must manage to function and survive in its immediate environment.

Following our three original research questions, we can propose the following responses and implications for further research. The question of how firms should behave in a position of the constant flux of global trends to assure sustainable growth in a regional context is a complex one; however, we can offer some tentative reference points. Research shows that the Open Innovation paradigm seems to be the most promising one that firms can embrace. Opening the boundaries and changing the attitude towards cooperation, and collaboration with in- and out- actors is a promising approach; in such cases, firms have to be ready to embrace changes in their business model. The most delicate is the aspect of knowledge management, encompassing IP management, but special care regarding intellectual capital (Chen et al., 2004) is also necessary. In such a context, our next research question was on whether the special organisational structure is necessary to be incorporated in the firm. Tentatively, we conclude that upscaling is necessary, apart from upscaling knowledge management; organisational structures, networks and evaluations processes also need to be upscaled (Chiaroni, 2011). Lastly, the third research question deals with the interplay of social forces inside and outside of organisations. It can be concluded that firms operate in social fields, constructed through the interplay of social forces of institutions, networks and cognitive frames. As such, firms are heavily influenced by the immediate cultural, political and economic environment; however, they have tools to influence, through their actions and participation in the market, the sustainable growth and development of the regions.

To sum up, as there was much work done in understanding the specific nuance of our main research problem, the main point of interest and departure for further research work remain in interest in positioning of firms with the Regional Innovation System. Further operationalisation and empirical work are suggested to support the theoretically proposed model of dynamics using SOFIA.

References

Amiri, A. N., Ramezan, M., and Omrani, A. (2010) 'Studying the Impacts of Organizational Organic Structure on Knowledge Productivity Effective Factors Case Study: Manufacturing Units in a Domestic Large Industrial Group', *European Journal of Scientific Research*, 40(1), 91–101.

Asheim, B. T., Grillitsch, M., and Trippl, M. (2016) 'Regional Innovation Systems: Past – Present – Future.' *Handbook on the Geographies of Innovation*, edited by Richard Shearmur, Christophe Carrincazeaux and David Doloreux. Cheltenham and Northampton: Edward Elgar.

Barnett, H. (1953) *Innovation*. New York: McGraw-Hill.

Barney, J. B. (1991) 'Firm Resources and Sustained Competitive Advantage', *Journal of Management*, 17(1), 99–120.

Becker, S. W., and Whistler, T. L. (1967) 'The Innovative Organization: A Selective View of Current Theory and Research', *The Journal of Business*, 40(1), 462–469.

Beckert, J. (2010) 'How Do Fields Change? The Interrelations of Institutions, Networks, and Cognition in the Dynamics of Markets', *Organization Studies*, 31(5), 605–27.

Besednjak Valič, T. (2019) 'Innovation, Digitalisation, and the HPC in the Danube Region.' In *Go with the Flow: High Performance Computing and Innovations in the Danube Region*, edited by Borut Rončević, Raluca Coscodaru, and Urška Fric. London, Budapest, Ljubljana: Vega Press, 22–46.

Besednjak Valič, T., Kolar, J., and Lamut, U. (2020). 'Three Scenarios of Innovation and Technology Transfer: The Case of Key Enabling Technologies in the Danube Region', *Journal of Engineering and Applied Sciences*, 15, 3619–3623.

Carroll, J. (1967) 'A Note on Departmental Autonomy and Innovation in Medical Schools', *The Journal of Business*, 40(1), 531–534.

Cepoi, V. (2019a) 'Interplay of Social Forces: A Focus on Regional Innovation Processes', *The Social Sciences*, 14(12), 423–430.

Cepoi, V. (2019b) 'Reshaping the Danube Region Imaginary: A Focus on Digital Transformation and HPC', *Research in Social Change*, 11(2), 58–78. DOI:10.2478/rsc-2019-0009.

Cepoi, V., and Golob, T. (2016) 'Regional Innovation Performance: Measuring Development in Cultural, Social and Economic Perspectives', *Innovative Issues and Approaches in Social Sciences*, 9(1), 242–60.

Cepoi, V., and Golob, T. (2017) 'Innovation Performance in the Eu Comparative Perspective: The Interplay of Social Forces in the Context of National Innovation Systems', *Comparative Sociology,* 16(4), 555–79.

Chen, J., Zhu, Z., and Xie, H. Y. (2004) 'Measuring Intellectual Capital: A New Model and Empirical Study', *Journal of Intellectual Capital*, 5(1), 195–212.

Chesbrough, H., and Crowther, A. K. (2006) 'Beyond High Tech: Early Adopters of Open Innovation in Other Industries', *R&D Management,* 36(3), 229–36.

Chiaroni, D., Chiesa, V., and Frattini, F. (2011) 'The Open Innovation Journey: How Firms Dynamically Implement the Emerging Innovation Management Paradigm', *Technovation,* 31(2011), 34–43.

Cooke, P., Uranga, M. G., and Etxebarria, G. (1997) 'Regional Innovation Systems: Institutional and Organisational Dimensions', *Research Policy,* 26(4), 475–91.

Cummings, S., Bridgman, T., and Brown, K. G. (2016) 'Unfreezing Change as Three Steps: Rethinking Kurt Lewin's Legacy for Change Management', *Human Relations*, 69(1), 33–60.

Doloreux, D., and Parto, S. (2005) 'Regional Innovation Systems: Current Discourse and Unresolved Issues', *Technology in Society,* 27(2), 133–53.

Drucker, P. F. (1985) *Innovation and Entrepreneurship.* New York, NY: Harper & Row.

Džajić Uršič, E. (2020) 'Systematized Analysis Using Data Mining's Methodology on the Topic of Regional Industrial Symbiosis and Its Networks', *Research in Social Change*, 12(3), 78–99. DOI:10.2478/rsc-2020-0011.

Fligstein, N., and McAdam, D. (2012) *A Theory of Fields*. New York: Oxford University Press.

Gangaliuc, C. (2019) 'The Measurement of Innovation for Management, Research and Policy', *Research in Social Change,* 11(2), 35–57. DOI:10.2478/rsc-2019-0008.

Gangaliuc, C., and Fric, U. (2019) 'National Case Study in the Danube Region: Montenegro.' In *Go with the Flow: High Performance Computing and Innovations in the Danube Region*, edited by Borut Rončević, Raluca Coscodaru, and Urška Fric. London: Vega Press.

Golob, T., and Makarovič, M., (2021) 'Sustainable Development through Morphogenetic Analysis: The Case of Slovenia', *Politics in Central Europe*, 17(1), 83–105.

Grant, R. M. (1991) 'A Resource-Based Theory of Competitive Advantage: Implications for Strategy Formulation', *California Management Journal*, 33(3), 114–135.

Hafner, A., and Modic, D. (2020) 'European Automotive Technological Innovation Systems in the Age of Disruption: The Suppliers' View', *Research in Social Change*, 12(3), 53–77. DOI:10.2478/rsc-2020-0014.

Isaken, A., and Trippl, M. (2016) 'Path Development in Different Regional Innovation Systems: A Conceptual Analysis.' In *Innovation Drivers and Regional Innovation Strategies*, edited by M. Davide Parrilli, Rune Dahl Fitjar, and Andrés Rodriguez-Pose, 66–85. New York and Abingdon: Routledge.

Kleindienst, P. (2017) 'Understanding the Different Dimensions of Human Dignity: Analysis of the Decision of the Constitutional Court of the Republic of Slovenia on the "Tito Street" Case', *DANUBE: Law and Economics Review*, 8/3, 117–137, doi: 10.1515/danb-2017-0009.

Kleindienst, P. (2019) 'Economic and Social Security in EU: Reforming Slovenian Law on Social Entrepreneurship', *Research in Social Change*, 11(2), 14–34. DOI: 10.2478/rsc-2019-0007.

Kleindienst, P., and Tomšič, M. (2017) 'Human Dignity as the Foundation of Democratic Political Culture: Legal and Philosophical Perspective', *Law, Culture and the Humanities*, 1–20, doi: 10.177/143872117738229.

Kleindienst, P., and Tomšič, M. (2018) 'Č lovekovo dostojanstvo kot del politične kulture v novih demokracijah: postkomunistična Slovenija', *Bogoslovni vestnik* 78(1), 159–172.

Knight, K. E. (1967) 'A Descriptive Model of the Intra-Firm Innovation Process', *Journal of Business*, 40(1), 478–496.

Lee, S., Park, G., Yoon, B., and Park, J. (2010) 'Open Innovation in SMEs – An Intermediated Network Model', *Research Policy*, 39(2), 290–300.

Ljubotina, Predrag (2020) 'The Influence of Entrepreneurial Skills, Educationa and Risk Perception on Career Choice Intent: The Case of European Students with Family Business Background', *Research in Social Change*, 12(3), 23–37. DOI:10.2478/rsc-2020-0002.

Lundvall, B. A., and Johnson, B. (2016) 'The Learning Economy'. In *The Learning Economy and the Economics of Hope*, edited by Bengt-Ake Lundvall, 107–130. London and New York: Anthem Press.

Majetić, F., Makarovič, M., Šimleša, D., and Golob, T. (2019) 'Performance of Work Integration Social Enterprises in Croatia, Slovenia, and Italian Regions of Lombardy and Trentino', *Economics & Sociology*, 12(1), 286–301.

Mansfield, E. (1963) 'Size of Firm, Market Structure and Innovation', *Journal of Political Economy*, 71(1), 556–576.

March, J. G. (1991) 'Exploration and Exploitation in Organizational Learning', *Organization Science*, 2(1), 71–87.

Martín de Castro, G., and López Sáez, P. (2008) 'Intellectual Capital in High-Tech Firms', *Journal of Intellectual Capital*, 9(1), 25–36.

Mattes, J. (2010) *Innovation in Multinational Companies: Organisational, Interorganisational and Regional Dilemmas*. Frankfurt am Main, Berlin, Bern, Bruxelles, New York, Oxford, Wien: Peter Lang.

Modic, D., and Damij, N. (2018) *Towards Intellectual Property Rights Management: Back-Office and Front-Office Perspectives*. Palgrave Macmillan.

Modic, D., and Rončević, B. (2018) 'Social Topography for Sustainable Innovation Policy: Putting Institutions, Social Networks and Cognitive Frames in Their Place', *Comparative Sociology*, 17(1), 100–127.

Naqshbandi, M. M., and Tabche, I. (2018) 'The Interplay of Leadership, Absorptive Capacity, and Organizational Learning Culture in Open Innovation: Testing a Moderated Mediation Model', *Technological Forecasting and Social Change* 133, 156–67.

Pandiloska Jurak, A. (2020) 'The Importance of High-Tech Companies for EU Economy: Overview and the EU Grand Strategies Perspective', *Research in Social Change*, 12(3): 32–52. DOI:10.2478/rsc-2020-0013.

Pandiloska Jurak (2018) A. 'Public Policy Instrument Evaluation in Service of Enabling Grand Strategy Discourse – Case of Horizon 202 Key Indicators', *Research in Social Change*, 11(2), 97–121. DOI:10.2478/rsc-2019-0011.

Pandiloska Jurak, A., and Pinterič, U. (2012) 'Assessment of Municipalities' Performances in Slovenia', *Transylvanian Review of Administrative Sciences*, (35), 121–137.

Perkmann, M., and Walsh, K. (2007) 'University–Industry Relationships and Open Innovation: Towards a Research Agenda', *International Journal of Management Reviews*, 9(4), 259–280.

Pezzi, M. (2007) 'Governance, Social Capital and Cultural Endowement as Important Factors in the Transformation of European Regions.' In *The Future of European Regions*, edited by Patrycja Jakubowska, Antoni Kuklinski, and Piotr Zuber, Vol. 1. Poland: Ministry of Regional Development Forum, REDEFO.

Pierce, J. L., and Delbecq, A. (1977) 'Organization Structure, Individual Attitudes and Innovation', *The Academy of Management Review*, 2(1), 27–37.

Ramezan, M. (2010) 'Intellectual Capital and Organizational Organic Structure in Knowledge Society: How Are These Concepts Related?', *International Journal of Information Management*, 31(2011), 88–95.

Robertson, P. L., Casali, G. L., and Jacobson, D. (2012) 'Managing Open Incremental Process Innovation: Absorptive Capacity and Distributed Learning', *Research Policy*, 41(5), 822–832.

Rončević, B. (2012) 'Regional Development Agencies and Changing Social Fields: Towards a Sociology of Regional Systems of Innovation'. In *Regional Development Agencies: The Next Generation?: Networking, Knowledge and Regional Policies*, edited by N. Bellini, M. Danson, and H. Halkier, 87–101. London; New York: Routledge.

Rončević, B. (2020) 'Technology and Innovations in Regional Development for Europe 2020: Jean Monnet Centre of Excellence TIR 2020 for Smart, Inclusive and Sustainable Growth', *Research in Social Change*, 12(3): 5–14. DOI:10.2478/rsc-2020-0011.

Rončević, B., and Besednjak Valič, T. (2019) 'How to Think about Regional Development Agencies as a Sociologist', *The Social Sciences*, 14(9), 326–34.

Rončević, B., and Makarovič, M. (2010) 'Towards the Strategies of Modern Societies: Systems and Social Processes', *Innovation: The European Journal of Social Science Research*, 23(3), 223–239.

Rončević, B., and Makarovič, M. (2011) 'Societal Steering in Theoretical Perspective: Social Becoming as an Analytical Solution', *Polish Sociological Review*, 176(4), 461–472.

Rončević, B., Makarovič, M., Tomšič, M., and Cepoi, V. (2018) 'Methodological Solutions for Comparative Research on Transformations.' In *The Routledge International Handbook of European Social Transformations*, edited by P. Vihalemm, A. Masso, and S. Opermann, 57–70. London and New York: Routledge.

Rončević, B., and Modic, D. (2011) 'Regional Systems of Innovations as Social Fields', *Sociologija i prostor: časopis za istraživanje prostornoga i sociokulturnog razvoja*, 49(191), 313–333.

Rončević, B., and Modic, D. (2012) 'Social Fields of Technological Innovations.' In *Global Trends and Regional Development*, edited by N. Genov, 226–247. New York: Routledge.

Rončević, Borut, Šušteršič, J., Wostner, P., and Besednjak Valič, T. (2010) 'Quo Vadis, Slovenia? Between Framework Conditions and Internal Capabilities', *Managing Global Transitions*, 8(4), 353–380.

Rončević, B., and Tomšič, M. (2017) 'Perspectives of Information Society: Bricolage of Manifestations.' In *Information Society and Its Manifestations: Economy, Politics, Culture*, edited by B. Rončević, and M. Tomšič, 9–21. Frankfurt am Main: Peter Lang.

Simard, C., and West, J. (2006) 'Knowledge Networks and the Geographical Locus of Innovation.' In *Open Innovation: Researching a New Paradigm*, edited by Henry Chesbrough, Wim Vanhaverbeke, and Joel West. Oxford and New York: Oxford University Press.

Spithoven, A., Clarysse, B., and Knockaert, M. (2010) 'Building Absorptive Capacity to Organise Inbound Open Innovation in Traditional Industries', *Technovation,* 30 (2), 130–41.

Vanhaverbeke, W., Van De Vrande, V., and Chesbrough, H. W. (2008) 'Understanding the Advantages of Open Innovation Practices in Corporate Venturing in Term of Real Options', *Creativity and innovation Management,* 17, 251–258.

Xia, T., and Roper, S. (2016) 'Unpacking Open Innovation: Absorptive Capacity, Exploratory and Exploitative Openness, and the Growth of Entrepreneurial Biopharmaceutical Firms', *Journal of Small Business Management,* 54 (3), 931–52.

Zobel, A. K. (2017) 'Benefiting from Open Innovation: A Multidimensional Model of Absorptive Capacity', *The Journal of Product Innovation Management',* 34(3), 269–288.

Urška Fric

Is Open Innovation (2.0) Leading to the Circular Economy (2.0)?

Abstract: This paper presents the role of the circular economy, which brings about an approach to include skills, knowledge, and tools to promote the sustainable use of natural resources, as well as producing sustainable products and services. We specifically focus on two new paradigms and their relationship – 'Circular Economy 2.0' (CE2) and 'Open Innovation 2.0' (OI2) – both as actions under ambitious EU policy – – CE2 as one of the actions for a cleaner and more competitive Europe and OI2 as one of the actions shaping Europe's digital future. Through an overview of the EU's ambitious policy, OI2 and CE2 at the EU level, and their relationship, we also present the OI2 and CE2 as crucial current paradigms and, where still needed, to increase up action at the EU level, providing the competitive advantage it brings to EU economy, close the loop, and to strengthen the framework supporting open innovation approaches. In addition to the two new paradigms and their relationship, this paper focuses on the *Europe 2020* strategy to present the status quo in the field of OI2 and CEI through monitoring progress towards the targets and goals defined under the three mutually reinforcing priorities – smart, sustainable and inclusive growth.

Keywords: Open innovation (2.0), circular economy (2.0), EU policies, Europe 2020, relationship

1. Introduction

As stated by the World Wildlife Fund, we live in a global economy that is exhausting natural capital: 'By 2012, the bio-capacity equivalent of 1.6 Earths was needed to provide the natural resources and services humanity consumed in that year' (WWF in De Angelis, 2018). Environmental care and quality are therefore central to our economy, our health and our well-being; however, it faces numerous issues, not least those of climate change, unsustainable consumption and production, waste disposal, as well as various forms of pollution (EUR-Lex, 2020). Effective waste management can also have an impact on the realisation of the human dignity of individuals (Kleindienst, 2017; Kleindienst and Tomšič, 2017; Kleindienst and Tomšič, 2018; Kleindienst, 2019).

Since its ambitious long-term grand strategies (e.g., Europe, 2020) also include goals of sustainable development (Makarovič et al., 2014), the European

Union (EU) has some of the world's highest environmental standards, developed over decades, which can be described as the most exhaustive modern standards compendium in all of the world (EUR-Lex, 2020). EU environmental and climate change legislation (also known as the environmental *acquis*) comprises over 500 directives, regulations, and decisions (EUR-Lex, 2020). EU environmental and climate change legislation protects natural habitats, keeps air and water clean, ensures proper waste disposal, improves knowledge about toxic chemicals, and helps businesses move toward a sustainable economy (EUR-Lex, 2020).

Design expertise is increasingly understood as relevant and useful in the development of government policy and strategy (Bason in Bailey, 2017) in the transformation from the linear to the circular economy. On the one hand, policymakers are responsible for deciding the direction for a productive dialogue between public and private entities (Nohra, 2018). The crucial role in decision-making offers them the opportunity to establish first impact measures and long-term vision that includes transforming public procurement policy, supplying financial or technical support to systemic-design-oriented industries, and generating collaboration platforms (Nohra, 2018). Eventually, these actions lead to a broader societal goal of encouraging a circular economy while creating synergies between the managing authorities, citizenship, and business (Nohra, 2018).

On the other hand, stakeholders in the global economy have been increasingly trying to keep up with environmental and climate change legislation and policies of the EU for the previous decade, resulting in the efficient handling of primary resources through reuse of waste in the domain of circular economy, which is the central the subject of this paper (Fric and Rončević, 2018: 121). This is becoming an increasingly complex and interdisciplinary issue (Mileva Boshkoska et al., 2018).

For the enforcement of the EU's policies, the transformation into a circular economy (i.e., closing the loop of products' lifecycles) is financially supported predominantly from the European Structural and Investment (ESI) Funds (2014–2020), the European Fund for Strategic Investments (EFSI), the LIFE programme and Horizon 2020 as the biggest EU Research and Innovation programme to date, from 2014 to 2020 (EC, 2020a). In addition to the private investment this money will attract, it promises more breakthroughs, discoveries, and world-firsts by taking great ideas from the lab to the market (EC, 2020a). Horizon 2020 is the financial instrument implementing the Innovation Union, a Europe 2020 flagship initiative to secure competitiveness in Europe, which is the main idea of Europe 2020, a strategy for smart, sustainable, and inclusive growth (EC, 2020a).

In 2015, the EC published a proposal ('Closing the Loop: Commission delivers on Circular Economy Action Plan') of new legislation on decreasing waste landfilling and increasing processing for reuse and recycling of the key waste flows – such as municipal and packaging waste (EUR-Lex, 2015). Over 50 actions under the 'Circular Economy Action Plan' launched in 2015 have been delivered or are being implemented in this period in the EU (Fric, 2019: 79). The 'Circular Economy Action Plan' also states that the new 'Small and Medium Enterprises (SMEs) Strategy' are going to foster circular industrial collaboration among SMEs building on training, advice under the 'Enterprise Europe Network' (EEN) on cluster collaboration, and on knowledge transfer via the 'European Resource Efficiency Knowledge Centre' (EREK) (European Cluster Collaboration Platform, 2020). As part of the governance of the sectorial actions, the EC will cooperate closely with stakeholders in key value chains to identify barriers to the expansion of markets for circular products and ways to address those barriers (ECCP, 2020). Building on the single market and the potential of digital technologies, the circular economy can strengthen the EU's industrial base and foster business creation and entrepreneurship among SMEs (ECCP, 2020).

For tracking and enforcement of transition from linear to the circular economy, cooperation is crucial in the field of knowledge and technology transfer and in the field of innovation (especially the latter) in practice and in the domain of this paper where we present the crucial paradigm of 'Open Innovation' 2.0 (OI2). In this paper. OI2 is understood as a new paradigm based on a 'Quadruple Helix Model' in which government, industry, academia, and civil stakeholders work together to co-create the future and drive structural changes far beyond the scope of what any one organisation or person could do alone (EC, 2020b): it is an ambitious effort at societal steering (Rončević and Makarovič, 2010, 2011). OI2 is a positive approach for innovation that helps to solve key European challenges by embracing change and not resisting it, financially supported predominantly from Europe the 2020 flagship initiative (EC, 2020b). For our purposes, we also understand OI2 as a complex model of innovation: OI2 is significantly more than a (conventional) linear model of the linkage from research to production without feedback paths within the ongoing work of development processes (Kline and Rosenberg, 2015: 28). OI2 is nowadays an innovation (Gangaliuc, 2019: 43–44) and an innovation system (Cepoi and Golob, 2017; Majetić et al., 2020; Besednjak Valič et al., 2020; Besednjak Valič, 2019; Cepoi, 2019: 59).

This paper first describes the legislative and legal framework in the Circular Economy (2.0) and Open Innovation (2.0). We predominantly use the concept of Ellen MacArthur Foundation (2016, 2017) to characterise the model of the circular economy as a response to the pressures of the growing economy, consumption of limited resources, and overall capacity of the environment. Second, we explicitly focus on two paradigms and their relationship (i.e., Circular Economy (2.0) and Open Innovation (2.0)), both of them as actions under ambitious EU policy. In the following, we present the overview of the relevant EU policies and status quo in the paradigms

2. Overview of the EU Policies

2.1 EU Environmental Policies: Circular Economy (2.0) from Past to Future

In the previous four decades, the EU's environmental policy has made huge strides: countries adopted a broad spectrum of environmental legislation, which can be described today as the most exhaustive modern standards compendium in the world (Fric, 2019: 79). As stated by the European Environment Agency (2011), policy initially focused on the development of a vast body of environmental legislation, dealing mostly with technical standards. Gradually, the spectrum of policy tools has broadened, with, for example, the introduction of market-based instruments.

The Ellen MacArthur Foundation (2020) emphasises the notion of circularity has deep historical and philosophical origins. The idea of feedback, of cycles in real-world systems, is ancient and has echoes in various schools of philosophy. It enjoyed a revival in industrialised countries after World War II when the advent of computer-based studies of non-linear systems unambiguously revealed the complex, interrelated, and therefore unpredictable nature of the world we live in: more akin to a metabolism than a machine. While the concept of a circular economy cannot be traced back to one single date or author, rather to different schools of thought (Wautelet, 2018: 2), legislative beginnings of the circular economy at the EU level predominantly dated in 2008.

In 2008 'Directive 2008/98/EC' proposed a new approach to waste handling and turning waste into raw materials and required EU members to adopt measures ensuring that as much waste as possible is reused in the future (EUR-Lex, 2008).

According to the worrisome status quo related to the low proportion of waste being recycled in Europe in 2014, the EC published a proposal of new legislation on recycling titled 'Towards a Circular Economy: A Zero Waste Programme for Europe' (EUR-Lex, 2014). The amendment intervened with a very complex and broad legislation framework on waste management, which had been in use in the EU for the previous four decades (EUR-Lex, 2014).

In 2015, the EC published a proposal ('Closing the loop: Commission delivers on Circular Economy Action Plan') of new legislation on decreasing waste landfills and increasing processing for the reuse and recycling of the key waste flows, such as municipal waste and packaging waste (EUR-Lex, 2015). Through the goals defined in the 'Circular Economy Action Plan', EU members would gradually achieve benchmarking results and encourage required investment in waste management (EUR-Lex, 2015). Effective waste management can have an impact on the realisation of the human dignity of individuals (Kleindienst, 2017; Kleindienst and Tomšič, 2017; Kleindienst and Tomšič, 2018; Kleindienst, 2019).

In the same year, the United Nations signed 'The Agenda 2030 for Sustainable Development and the Sustainable Development Goals', in which one of the 17 goals focuses on implementing sustainable production and consumption methods (WHO, 2016: 2–3). The deadline for all goals is set for 2030; however, the most important characteristic of this agenda is its universality (WHO, 2016: 2–3). Considering national specifics, its goals are attainable by all countries, whether they are developed or still in the development phase (WHO, 2016: 2–3).

In 2017, the EC published a communiqué and working document titled 'Strengthening Innovation in Europe's Regions: Strategies for Resilient, Inclusive and Sustainable Growth of the Commission's Committees'. The document described the proposed development of smart specialisation while tackling the following main challenges (EC, 2017): boosting the innovation and competitiveness potential of European regions as a basis for a sustainable growth model; increasing interregional cooperation, which is a key element in globalised economies; strengthening the focus on less developed and industrial transition regions; improving and building on joint work across EU policies and programmes supporting innovation.

In 2018, the EC (2019a) signed the 'Circular Economy Action Plan', which involved numerous new strategies, measures and suggestions concerning managing the complete lifecycle of plastics from design to recycling for the whole EU, requiring that all plastic packaging is recyclable by 2030. For this to happen, EU countries would have to develop new cost-efficient and effective methods of plastic recycling, reduce plastic packaging altogether, and increase investments in this area to provide innovative approaches (EC, 2019a). To reduce marine litter originating from the sea, the EC demanded that port receptions use oxo-degradable plastic.

Later in 2018, the EC adopted some additional ambitious initiatives (EC, 2019a): (1) proposal of legislation considering reducing the environmental impact of certain plastic products, which would present the implementation phase of the EU-wide strategy for adopting circular economy on plastics, and (2) proposal of minimum requirements regarding water reuse to ensure stable, safe, economically viable and efficient reuse of water for irrigation.

In 2019, the EC published: (1) a report on 'Recovery of Critical and Other Raw Materials from Mining and Landfills', (2) 'Guidance on Best Practices in Extractive Waste Management', and (3) adopted its '4th Circular Economy Package' including an implementation report covering the full 'Circular Economy Action Plan' (EC, 2019b).

At the beginning of March 2020, the EC adopted 'Circular Economy Package 2.0', one of the main building blocks of the 'European Green Deal', Europe's new agenda for smart, sustainable and inclusive growth (EC, 2020c). With measures along the entire life cycle of products, the new 'Circular Economy Package Plan' aims to make our economy fit for a green future, strengthen our competitiveness while protecting the environment and give consumers new rights (European Commission, 2020c). Building on the work done since 2015, it focuses on the design and production for a circular economy, intending to ensure that the resources used are kept in the EU economy for as long as possible (EC, 2020c). The 'Circular Economy Package Plan' and the initiatives therein are going to be developed with the close involvement of the business and stakeholder community (EC, 2020c).

2.2 EU Policies on Open Innovation (2.0): A Paradigm for Shaping Europe's Digital Future

In 2013, the EC (2013, p. 4) emphasised that open innovation is used as a synonym for modern, highly dynamic, and interactive processes in the European context. Linear and sequential mindsets are slowly changing to be more opportunistic, more daring, and more action-oriented. In the EU, we need to move from having 'perfect plans for yesterday' to an innovation culture that fosters experimentation and prototyping in real-world settings. This innovation culture leads to simultaneous technological and societal innovation and encouragement. We need to be daring and experiment with disruptive approaches as gradual improvement does not properly reflect the potential that the omnipresent, fast-developing information communication technologies (ICT) provide parallel innovations.

Seven years later, in 2020, the EC launched the strategy 'Shaping Europe's Digital Future'. Over the next five years, it is going to focus on three key digital objectives (EC, 2020d; Tosdevin, 2020):

❖ technology that works for people;
❖ a fair and competitive economy;
❖ an open, democratic and sustainable society.

The strategy 'Shaping Europe's Digital Future' is one of the priorities under 'A Europe Fit for the Digital Age: Empowering People with a New Generation of Technologies', which aims to make transformation work for people and businesses while helping to achieve its target of a climate-neutral Europe by 2050 (EC, 2020d). One of the activities under the mentioned strategy is 'Open Innovation 2.0' (OI2) as a positive approach for innovation that helps solve key European challenges by embracing change and not resisting it (EC, 2020b).

As stated by Curley and Salmelin (2013: 2), 'Open Innovation 2.0' (OI2) is a paradigm based on principles of integrated collaboration, co-created shared value, cultivated innovation ecosystems, unleashed exponential technologies, and extraordinarily rapid adoption. The adoption of the OI2 paradigm will be the catalyst that unleashes a virtual 'Cambrian Explosion' of innovation in Europe. Instead of gravitating to the lowest common denominator of its society, Europeans will deliver to the highest common multiple by leveraging all the talents and resources of European society. OI2 is all about an openness to innovation that does not resist change but embraces it. OI2 requires a new mindset focused on teams, collaboration, and sharing. Only with this focus will it be possible to tear down the walls that form separate silos of civil, academic, business, and government innovation. Silos will be replaced with creative commons, shared social capital, and the systematic harvesting of experimental results. Information technology (IT) is going to play a crucial role in the process of 'networkisation' (Rončević and Tomšič, 2017); it can supply the necessary connectivity and enable social networking among innovators and the communities they serve (Curley and Salmelin, 2013: 2).

As mentioned above and as explicitly stated by the EC (2020), OI2 as a paradigm based on a 'Quadruple Helix Model' in which government, industry, academia and civil stakeholders work together to co-create the future and drive structural changes far beyond the scope of what any one organisation or person could do alone. This model also encompasses user-oriented innovation models to take full advantage of ideas' cross-fertilisation leading to experimentation and prototyping in a real-world setting. In the field are the following five crucial elements in the 'Open Innovation Process':

❖ networking;
❖ collaboration – involving partners, competitors, universities, and users;
❖ corporate entrepreneurship – enhancing corporate venturing, start-ups and spin-offs;
❖ proactive intellectual property management (IPR) – creating new markets for technology;
❖ research and development (R&D) – achieving competitive advantages in the market.

The EC bases its thinking on a 'Quadruple Helix Model' involving institutional bodies, the research sphere, the business sector, and citizens in the process. This new generation of open innovation leads to stronger economic impact and better user experience in Europe (EC, 2020b). In the following, we clarify the role of the circular economy and open innovation for the EU (global) economy through crucial concepts and theory.

3. Some Theoretical Concepts: Circular Economy (2.0) and Open Innovation (2.0)

3.1 Circular Economy (2.0)

The circular economy concept and terminology has gained momentum since the 2012 World Economic Forum, where this report, prepared in collaboration with the Ellen MacArthur Foundation and McKinsey & Company, showed for the first time its convenience and the way to drive a new economic development (World Economic Forum in Barbero, 2017: 9). As emphasised by the Ellen MacArthur Foundation (2016, 2017), the circular economy is the EU's way of dealing with the pressures of growing economies and consumption on limited resources and environmental capacity as one of its most highly developed concepts. Therefore, the metamorphosis into a circular economy is based on the re-use, adaptation, and processing of existing materials and products. To minimise waste production, it also allows for using more renewable energy sources, discontinuing hazardous chemicals, cutting down on raw material, and reinventing product design to make it more recyclable and still retain its added value for as long as possible. In a circular economy, products remain in the environment even after they have reached the end of their lifespan.

As the Ellen MacArthur Foundation (2016) summarises, the circular economy can be defined from different aspects. In its essence, it presents a global model of sustainable economic development in which resources are used moderately and reasonably. From a resource point-of-view, the model discriminates between biological and technical materials and results in prolonging the useful lifespan of both as much as possible. In the pre-manufacturing phase, the circular economy model requires that products be designed effectively and efficiently to enable their circular flow. Regarding economic opportunities, it stimulates innovative approaches to all stages of product lifespan and, by providing all of the above, it sets a course for a new sustainable system. The linear economy is observable by its straightforward flow downwards, while the circular economy is depicted in the form of loops, representing the bilateral flow of different materials (Webster, 2017: 18).

The circular economy system diagram depicts three stages: (1) the goal of the first stage is to retain and fortify natural capital by controlling the limited resources and harmonising the renewable resource flows; (2) the second stage focuses on improving the profitability of resources through the circulation of products, components, and materials being used; its goal was to make the products, components, and materials as useful as possible in every phase of technological or natural cycles: (3) the last stage in the diagram wishes to increase the system's efficiency by opening the system and restructuring it in such way to avoid negative external expense (Fric, 2019: 84).

In the business world, various models and standards based on specific criteria and methodological tools measure and value quality, effectiveness, efficiency and excellence (Pandiloska Jurak and Pinterič, 2012). In the process of applying the circular economy into practice, certain concepts are being put in place. One such tool is Cradle-to-Cradle®, a registered trademark of McDonough Braungart Design Chemistry, LLC (C2C-Centre, 2013). It ensures the quality of resources through its multiple lifecycles, whereas all resources must be manufactured from nontoxic materials and return to the manufacturing process of the same stakeholder once their lifespan expires (C2C-Centre, 2013). Another tool is industrial symbiosis, which has become an extremely important sustainable mechanism for the recycling of waste in industrial and non-industrial processes over the previous two decades. We can, therefore, understand it as a relationship between three or more social stakeholders, which are linked through direct exchange of material, while the exchanges between stakeholders present synergies (Rončević and Fric, 2015: 37; Fric et al. 2020: 2). In the domain of industrial symbiosis as a paradigm of connecting flows (Džajić Uršič and Rončević, 2017: 71; also Džajić Uršič, 2020) are another two various ways we can reuse waste and other discarded materials: upcycling and downcycling. While upcycling and downcycling are both examples of recycling, not all recycling is considered equal (Looptworks, 2015). When we convert discarded materials into something of equal or greater value, it is 'upcycled' (Looptworks, 2015). When a material or product is 'downcycled', it is transformed into something of lesser value (Looptworks, 2015).

The EC unveiled its 'New Circular Economy Action Plan' (also known as 'Circular Economy 2.0') in March 2020, confirming the EU's intention of halving municipal waste by 2030, and suggesting that consumers have a new 'right to repair' for computers and smartphones (Simon, 2020). The EC (2020e) states that it introduces legislative and non-legislative measures targeting areas where action at the EU level brings real added value. The CE2 presents measures to (EC, 2020 e): (1) make sustainable products the norm in the EU; (2) empower consumers and public buyers; (3) focus on the sectors that use most resources and where the potential for circularity is high; (4) ensure less waste; (5) make circularity work for people, regions and cities; and (6) lead global efforts on circular economy.

3.2 Open Innovation (2.0)

'Open Innovation' is a term promoted by Henry Chesbrough, professor and executive director at the 'Center for Open Innovation at University of California', Berkeley, in his book 'Open Innovation: 'The New Imperative for Creating and Profiting from Technology' in 2003 (EURIS, 2012). Chesbrough (2003 in EURIS, 2012) defines 'Open Innovation' as a new paradigm that assumes organisations can and should use external ideas and internal ideas and internal and external paths to market, as the organisations look to advance their technology.

While 'Open Innovation' is a model based on the thought that organisations can benefit from the free bi-directional flow of ideas and innovations from both within and outside the organisation, 'Open Innovation 2.0' is (OI2) much more than a version of open innovation (Morikawa, 2016).

As mentioned above and as Morikawa (2016) writes, OI2 is a model that challenges the traditional internally focused research and development (R&D) innovation funnel where benefits have been noted as far back as the 1960s. Previously, organisations tended to innovate strictly within their organisation and have little or no collaboration with external stakeholders. Open innovation suggested that innovation funnels should be open to ideas from external sources and be prepared to let go of some of the ideas on which the organisation will not focus. This meant that organisations started to collaborate with start-ups and other external stakeholders. In this collaboration model, bigger organisations typically work with and fund start-ups to learn from and potentially acquire the start-ups if the business starts to look promising enough. Open innovation projects take all ideas into account; even if a certain idea cannot be used in the context of a certain project, it might still be applicable somewhere by someone else, emphasises Morikawa (2016).

According to Morikawa (2016), following this initial version, open innovation has developed significantly; recently, an aspiring new model, OI2, has gradually gained steam. This model challenges organisations with a vision of even more open collaboration with a vision of many organisations and individuals working together in a network setting. In OI2, innovation happens in ecosystems or networks that go far beyond traditional organisational boundaries. In OI2 can be several organisations, individuals, universities, and governments collaborating with one another; together, the network can create value in a way no organisation could do by itself. There are always many different innovation funnels present in a single OI2 network due to the sheer number of stakeholders involved. Some of these funnels might be in the same organisations, but some are not; this inter-funnel collaboration is the source of much of the synergies present in the model: it creates diversity in innovation (Morikawa, 2016; Golob and Makarovič, 2021).

Morikawa (2016) also writes that the OI2 model emphasises the diversity of the collaborators. Evidence showing diversity and multidisciplinarity in innovation is likely to result in both the highest and lowest quality outcomes. One of the reasons for this is that in a more diverse setting, people feel more at ease to share their thoughts and ideas; thus, if the organisation wants to maximise its chances of creating breakthrough innovations, it must embrace diversity. The author states one of the obvious methods for creating openness and facilitating this kind of diversity is to create environments, such as open facilities or campuses. These kinds of spaces allow unlikely people to meet, resulting in new ideas and innovations. The spatial collaboration might be a good starting point but usually is not enough. Having the kind of technology that we do, networks often interact mostly without the limitations of physical space. Hence, innovative environments include all kinds of 'virtual' platforms which they use to activate and involve their stakeholders' community, summarises the author. In the following, we present the relationship between the circular economy (2.0) and open innovation (2.0) at the EU level through best practices.

3.3 Circular Economy (2.0) and Open Innovation (2.0): Their Relationship through Best Practices

Luis Rodriguez (2020) from Ennmotive (an 'Open Innovation Hub for Engineering') emphasises when talking about the circular economy, what first comes to mind sometimes is to recover the energy contained in the waste generated anywhere. The recovery of such energy (also known as 'Waste to Energy') consists of controlled combustion that generates thermal energy, later transformed into electric power. Although this process is already successfully developed and well implemented in countries like the Netherlands, Sweden or China, not all the waste has heating value or can undergo sustainable combustion. As mentioned previously, waste can be reused for creating new products and creating new sources of revenue. According to Rodriguez (2020), the relationship between the circular economy (2.0) and open innovation (2.0) is seen through the following examples of best practices in the field of mining and manufacturing.

In the first example, Rodriguez (2020) explains that mining generates large amounts of waste that ends up in tailing dams, which generates a serious environmental problem. In 2018, the organisation 'Ennmotive' launched a circular economy competition to help a leading organisation to find solutions to the mine tailing challenge. The goal of the competition was to find marketable applications for their waste, mainly composed of silica and smaller amounts of titanium oxide, calcium oxide, magnesium oxide, aluminium oxide, among others. The challenge was to repurpose as much waste as possible, with the lowest reprocessing. One of the reasons is reprocessing low metal concentration waste is generally not cost-efficient. This challenge grabbed the interest of many engineers and attracted over 70 participants. As a result, both brand new applications and existing ones were submitted and now, the two winning proposals are under development. The winners were organisation 'Oliver Loidi', from France, and the organisation 'Cliff Edwards', from Canada, who brought new revenue opportunities for the clean energy and oil and gas sectors (Rodriguez, 2020).

In the second example of a best practice, Rodriguez (2020) cites Masisa, a manufacturer of different types of boards that are cut by distributors and other clients to make furniture and other products. The cutting process generates waste, which is sent to sanitary landfills where its recovery potential value is lost. Since these board parts had chemical components that did not allow their direct combustion, the organisation turned to 'Ennmotive' to launch an open innovation challenge to look for new solutions. Consequently, the goal of the challenge was to repurpose this wood waste to manufacture new products, create revenue and reduce the environmental impact. One of the solutions that resulted from this challenge was the use of the board scraps to make recyclable wooden cutlery as an alternative to plastic. However, the business case was not so attractive. Finally, the winning solution was to manufacture innovative tiles for affordable housing. This product was a low-cost, durable and aesthetically pleasing alternative to the traditional metal roof. The winner of this challenge was the mechanical engineer Michael Ankobia, from the United Kingdom, with experience in a wide range of engineering fields.

Rodriguez (2020) summarises many organisations are using open innovation (2.0) to obtain better results in their circular economy (2.0) initiatives. It is relatively clear that open innovation (2.0) leads to a circular economy (2.0).

4. Conclusion

In 2019, the EC (2019a) noted that the circular economy (2.0) is an irreversible, global trend, but much remains needed to scale up action at the EU level and globally, to close the loop fully and to provide the competitive advantage it brings to the EU economy. Increased efforts will be needed to implement the revised waste legislation and develop markets for secondary raw materials. The work started at the EU level on some issues needs to be accelerated if Europe wants to reap the full benefit of a transition to a circular economy and still EC notes (EC, 2019a).

Interaction with different stakeholders suggests some areas not yet covered by the 'Circular Economy Action Plan (2.0)' could be investigated to complete the agenda. One of these areas is undoubtedly 'Open Innovation (2.0)' as a crucial driver or method for the transition from a linear to a circular economy (evidenced by successful examples of best practices in Europe).

As stated by Curley and Salmelin (2013), it is noteworthy that Europe is traditionally stronger in research output and weaker in innovation take-up. To improve adoption rates, new ambitious EU policies stress a more holistic perspective for research, development, and innovation (RD&I); this is another step in the right direction. These ambitious EU policies should encourage more Europeans to take measured risks and reap the benefits of new higher-expectation businesses.

References

Bailey, J. (2017). Elements of Novelty: Designer as Policy-Maker. In: Barbero, S. (ed.): *Systemic Design Method Guide for Policymaking: A Circular Europe on the Way.* Torino: Umberto Allemandi srl. : 43–50.

Barbero, S. (2017): Systemic Design Method Guide for Policymaking. A Circular Europe on the Way. Torino: Umberto Allemandi srl.: 9–12.

Besednjak Valič, T. (2019). Innovation, Digitalisation, and the HPC in the Danube Region. In: B. Roncevic, R. Coscodaru and U. Fric eds. *Go with the Flow: High Performance Computing and Innovations in the Danube Region*. London, Budapest, Ljubljana: Vega Press Ltd.: 22–46.

Besednjak Valič, T., Kolar, J., and Lamut, U. (2020). Three Scenarios of Innovation and Technology Transfer: The Case of Key Enabling Technologies in the Danube Region. *Journal of Engineering and Applied Sciences*. 15: 3619–3623.

Cepoi, V. (2019). Reshaping the Danube Region Imaginary: A Focus on Digital Transformation and HPC. *Research in Social Change* 11(2): 58–78. DOI:10.2478/rsc-2019-0009.

Cepoi, V. and Golob, T. (2017). Innovation Performance in the Eu Comparative Perspective: The Interplay of Social Forces in the Context of National Innovation Systems. *Comparative Sociology*. 16(4): 555–79.

C2C-Centre. (2013). World First: First Impact Measurement Cradle to Cradle. Retrieved 07.03.2020 from http://www.c2c-centre.com/news/world-first-first-impactmeasurement-cradle-cradle.

Curley, M. and Salmelin, B. (2013). Open Innovation 2.0: A New Paradigm. OI2 Conference Paper. Retrieved 03.03.2020 from https://uc-dk.dk/uasnet/wp-content/uploads/Open-Innovation-2.0-Salmelin.pdf.

De Angelis, R. (2018). Business Models in the Circular Economy. Concepts, Examples and Theory. Cham: Palgrave Pivot: 1.

Džajić Uršič, E. (2020). Systematized Analysis Using Data Mining's Methodology on the Topic of Regional Industrial Symbiosis and Its Networks. *Research in Social Change*, 12(3), 78–99. DOI:10.2478/rsc-2020-0011.

Džajić Uršič, E. and Rončević, B. (2017). Industrial Symbiotic Networks in the Information Society: Research Challenges and Perspectives. In: Rončević, B. and Tomšič, M. (eds.): *Information Society and Its Manifestations: Economy, Politics, Culture*. Frankfurt am Main: PL Academic Research: 71–81.

Ellen MacArthur Foundation. (2016). Circular Economy Overview. Retrieved 12.02.2020 from https://www.ellenmacarthurfoundation.org/circular-economy/overview/concept.

Ellen MacArthur Foundation. (2017). Circular Economy Overview. Retrieved 12.02.2020 from https://www.ellenmacarthurfoundation.org/circular-economy/overview/concept.

Ellen MacArthur Foundation. (2020). Concept. What is a Circular Economy? A Framework an Economy that is Restorative and Regenerative by Design. Retrieved 13.02.2020 from https://www.ellenmacarthurfoundation.org/circular-economy/concept.

EURIS. (2012). Embracing Open Innovation in Europe. Retrieved 16.02.2020 from https://wrs.region-stuttgart.de/uploads/media/publikationen_euris_guide.pdf.

EUR-Lex. (2008). Access to European Law. Directive 2008/98/EC of the European Parliament and of the Council of 19 November 2008 on Waste and repealing certain Directives. Retrieved 13.02.2020 from http://eur-lex.europa.eu/legalcontent/EN/TXT/PDF/?uri=CELEX:32008L0098&from=EN.

EUR-Lex. (2014). Access to European Law. Communication from the Commission to the European Parliament, the Council, the European Economic and Social Committee and the Committee of the Regions towards a Circular Economy: A Zero Waste Programme for Europe. Retrieved 13.02.2020 from http://eur-lex.europa.eu/legalcontent/EN/TXT/PDF/?uri=CELEX:52014DC0398&from=EN.

EUR-Lex. (2015). Access to European Law. Communication from the Commission to the European Parliament, the Council, the European Economic and Social Committee and the Committee of the Regions Closing the Loop: An EU Action Plan for the Circular Economy. 2015, retrieved 13.02.2020 from http://eur-lex.europa.eu/legal-content/EN/TXT/?uri=CELEX:52015DC0614.

EUR-Lex. (2020a). Access to European Law. Communication from the Commission to the European Parliament, the Council, the European Economic and Social Committee and the Committee of the Regions Closing the Loop: An EU Action Plan for the Circular Economy. Retrieved 11.02.2020, from http://eur-lex.europa.eu/legal-content/EN/TXT/?uri=CELEX:52015DC0614.

EUR-Lex. (2020b). Access to European Law. Summaries of EU Legislation. Environment and Climate Change. Retrieved 06.02.2020, from https://eur lex.europa.eu/summary/chapter/environment.html?root_default=SUM_1_CODED%3D20&locale=en.

European Cluster Collaboration Platform. (2020). New Circular Economy Action Plan supports a Green Future for Europe through the Circular Economy Transition. Retrieved 10.02.2020, from https://www.clustercollaboration.eu/news/new-circular-economy-action-plan-supports-green-future-europe-through.

European Commission. (2013). Open Innovation 2.0. Open Innovation. Retrieved 28.02.2020 from https://www.urenio.org/wp-content/uploads/2008/11/2013-Open-Innovation-Yearbook-2013.pdf.

European Commission. (2014). Open Innovation 2.0. Yearbook 2014. Retrieved 14.03.2020 from https://www.researchgate.net/publication/277007320_The_Open_Innovation_20_Yearbook_2014.

European Commission. (2017). Strengthening Innovation in Europe's Regions: Strategies for Resilient, Inclusive and Sustainable Growth of the Commission's Committees. Retrieved 15.02.2020, from https://ec.europa.eu/regional_policy/sources/docoffic/2014/com_2017_376_2_en.pdf.

European Commission. (2019a). Circular Economy. Implementation of the Circular Economy Action Plan. Retrieved 15.02.2020, from https://ec.europa.eu/environment/circular-economy/index_en.htm.

European Commission. (2019b). Internal Market, Industry, Entrepreneurship and SMEs. Retrieved 15.02.2020, from https://ec.europa.eu/growth/industry/sustainability/circular-economy_en.

European Commission. (2020a). What is Horizon 2020? Retrieved 10.02.2020, from https://ec.europa.eu/programmes/horizon2020/what-horizon-2020.

European Commission. (2020b). Open Innovation 2.0. Retrieved 11.02.2020 from https://ec.europa.eu/digital-single-market/en/open-innovation-20.

European Commission. (2020c). Changing How We Produce and Consume: New Circular Economy Action Plan Shows the Way to a Climate-neutral, Competitive Economy and Empowered Consumers. Retrieved 11.03.2020 from https://ec.europa.eu/commission/presscorner/detail/en/ip_20_420.

European Commission. (2020d). A Europe Fit for the Digital Age: Empowering People with a new Generation of Technologies. Retrieved 01.03.2020 from https://ec.europa.eu/info/strategy/priorities-2019-2024/europe-fit-digital-age_en.

European Commission. (2020e). EU Circular Economy Action Plan. A New Circular Economy Action Plan for a Cleaner and More Competitive Europe. Retrieved 13.03.2020 from https://ec.europa.eu/environment/circular-economy/.

European Environment Agency. (2011). A Europe of Firsts: Environmental Achievements. Retrieved, 13.02.2020, from https://www.eea.europa.eu/environmental-time-line/a-europe-of-firsts-environmental-achievements.

Fric, U. (2019). Impact of Circular Economy as the EU's Ambitious Policy. *Research in Social Change*. 11(2): 79–96. DOI:10.2478/rsc-2019-0010.

Fric, U. and Rončević, B. (2018). E-Simbioza: Leading the Way to a Circular Economy through Industrial Symbiosis in Slovenia. *Socijalna ekologija*. 27(2): 119–140, retrieved 07.02.2020. DOI: 10.17234/SocEkol.27.2.1.

Fric, U., Rončević, B. and Džajić, Uršič, E. (2020). Role of Computer Software Tools in Industrial Symbiotic Networks and the Examination of Sociocultural Factors. *Environmental Progress & Sustainable Energy*. 39(2): 1–7.

Gangaliuc, C. (2019). The Measurement of Innovation for Management, Research and Policy. *Research in Social Change.* 11(2): 35–57. DOI:10.2478/rsc-2019-0008.

Golob, T. and Makarovič, M. (2021). Sustainable Development through Morphogenetic Analysis: The Case of Slovenia. *Politics in Central Europe.* 17(1): 83–105.

Kleindienst, P. (2017). Understanding the Different Dimensions of Human Dignity: Analysis of the Decision of the Constitutional Court of the Republic of Slovenia on the "Tito Street" Case. *DANUBE: Law and Economics Review.* 8(3): 117–137, doi: 10.1515/danb-2017-0009.

Kleindienst, P. (2019). Zgodovinski temelji sodobne paradigme človekovega dostojanstva. *Phainomena.* 28(108–109): 259–282, doi: 10.32022/PHI28.2019.108-109.11.

Kleindienst, P. and Tomšič, M. (2017). Human Dignity as the Foundation of Democratic Political Culture: Legal and Philosophical Perspective. *Law, Culture and the Humanities.* 1–20, doi: 10.177/143872117738229.

Kleindienst, P. and Tomšič, M. (2018). Človekovo dostojanstvo kot del politične kulture v novih demokracijah: postkomunistična Slovenija. *Bogoslovni vestnik.* 78 (1): 159–172.

Kline, Stephen, J. and Rosenberg, N. (2015). An Overview of Innovation. In: Suzigan, W. and Garcia, R. (eds.): *Brazilian Journal of Innovation.* 14(1): 17–47.

Looptworks. (2015). Upcycling, Downcycling and Recycling Explained. Retrieved 09.03.2020 from https://www.looptworks.com/blogs/looptworks-blog/34391171-upcycling-downcycling-and-recycling-explained.

Majetić, F., Makarovič, M., Šimleša, D. and Golob, T. (2019). Performance of Work Integration Social Enterprises in Croatia, Slovenia, and Italian Regions of Lombardy and Trentino. *Economics and sociology.* 12(1): 286–301.

Makarovič, M., Šušteršič, J. and Rončević, B. (2014). Is Europe 2020 Set to Fail?: The Cultural Political Economy of the EU Grand Strategies. *European Planning Studies*, 22(3): 610–626.

Mileva Boshkoska, B., Rončević, B. and Džajić Uršič, E. (2018). Modeling and Evaluation of the Possibilities of Forming a Regional Industrial Symbiosis Networks. *Social Sciences*, 7(1), 13. DOI: 10.3390/socsci7010013.

Morikawa, M. (2016). What Is Open Innovation 2.0 and Why Does It Matter? Retrieved 15.03.2020 from https://www.viima.com/blog/what-is-open-innovation-2.0-and-why-does-it-matter.

Nohra, C. G. (2018). Introduction. In: Pallaro, A. and Pereno, A. (eds.): *Good Practices Guide. Systemic Approaches for a Circular Economy*. Torino: Umberto Allemandi srl.: 7–10.

Pandiloska Jurak, A. and Pinterič, U. (2012). Assessment of Municipalities' Performances in Slovenia. *Transylvanian Review of Administrative Sciences*. (35): 121–137.

Rodriguez, L. (2020). Circular Economy and Open Innovation. Retrieved 18.03.2020 from https://www.ennomotive.com/circular-economy-open-innovation/.

Rončević, B. and Fric, U. (2015). Researching Industrial Symbiosis: Challenges and Dilemmas. In: Povh, J. (ed.): *Applied Modelling and Computing in Social Science*. Frankfurt am Main: PL Academic Research: 35–49.

Rončević, B. and Makarovič, M. (2010). Towards the Strategies of Modern Societies: Systems and Social Processes. *Innovation: The European Journal of Social Science Research*, 23(3): 223–239.

Rončević, B. and Makarovič, M. (2011). Societal Steering in Theoretical Perspective: Social Becoming as an Analytical Solution. *Polish Sociological Review*, 176(4): 461–472.

Rončević, B. and Tomšič, M. (2017). Perspectives of Information Society: Bricolage of Manifestations. In: Rončević, B. and Tomšič, M. (eds.): *Information Society and Its Manifestations: Economy, Politics, Culture*. Frankfurt am Main: Peter Lang: 9–21.

Simon, F. (2020). EU Unveils Circular Economy Plan 2.0, Drawing Mixed Reactions. Retrieved 13.03.2020 from https://www.euractiv.com/section/circular-economy/news/eu-unveils-circular-economy-plan-2-0-drawing-mixed-reactions/.

Tosdevin, A. (2020). European Commission Unveils Strategy for Shaping Europe's Digital Future. Retrieved 01.03.2020 from https://www.lexology.com/library/detail.aspx?g=bfe1dd00-5c96-4ec6-86ba-e7402b1bc21e.

Wautelet, T. (2018). The Concept of Circular Economy: Its Origins and its Evolutions. Working Paper. Retrieved 13.02.2020 from https://www.researchgate.net/publication/322555840_The_Concept_of_Circular_Economy_its_Origins_and_its_Evolution/link/5a5fcd1a458515b4377b840c/download.

World Health Organization (WHO). (2016). A Healthy Link: The Protocol on Water and Health and the Sustainable Development Goals. Retrieved 13.02.2020 from https://www.unece.org/fileadmin/DAM/env/water/mop4/Informal_doc/1623151_E_FinalWEB_rev.pdf.

Technologies, Innovations and Regional Policy

Alenka Pandiloska Jurak

Technologies, Innovation and Regional Policy – It Is Not All About Business

Abstract: The European Union is an entity of broad differences. Its regions are not progressing equally. Not all have the same starting possibilities in the form of existing infrastructure, budget availability, income levels, business culture; the regions also have different developmental policies, among other factors. Also, even rich regions have sub-regions with local issues that can be quite similar to those in less developed EU regions and countries in general. In a time of economic growth, companies seek new technologies and innovation, which is accompanied by the need to find skilled workers. If there are none in the nearby area, companies must consider how to attract and attain workers from elsewhere. They are not alone in this, because it has become generally known and confirmed by research that in the time of economic growth, the workers do not only follow the flow of money. Living conditions, cultural events, sports facilities, housing, general living standards – which of these factors comes first? Not all cities and towns can have higher education institutions, cultural infrastructure, and decision-making institutions. The question of how to attract and attain workers might be simple, but the answer is complex, starting on the level of policies. What is required is not 'a policy' but 'co-dependent policies': smart specialisation, regional development, infrastructure, culture, health, education (primary up to higher education). Policies and actions take time, money, and effort on local, regional, and national levels. To address the issue, the workers and what motivates them to move to a different place must be understood.

Keywords: technologies; innovations; regional policy; European Union; Europe 2020

1. Steering the EU towards Technology and Innovation Force

The Europe 2020 grand strategy, despite all inherent weaknesses (Makarovič et al., 2014), together with its strategy of smart specialisation and an extensive financial support programme, Horizon 2020 for EU research and innovation, set the course, which also shapes the next, Europe 2030 policies. As Foray says (2014, 1–101), the notion of smart specialisation describes the capacity of an economic system to generate new specialities through the discovery of new domains of opportunity and the local concentration and agglomeration of resources and competences in these domains. Given the complex nature of the development of contemporary societies (Adam et al., 2005), this kind of capacity is needed to initiate structural changes in diversification, transition, modernisation, or the radical foundation of industries and/or services (ibid).

The smart specialisation concept is now a major driving force behind both the new 'Innovation Union' flagship programme of the European Commission and the EU cohesion policy reforms (McCann and Ortega-Argilés, 2015, 2–12). McCann and Ortega-Argilés explain (ibid.) that the Innovation Union initiative aims to foster the dissemination and the realisation of EU-wide economies of scale in high-technology and knowledge-intensive sectors, while the EU cohesion policy aims to promote the development of many of Europe's weaker regions. These aims may appear to be somewhat incompatible, but how the smart specialisation concept is being applied in Europe potentially allows for both sets of objectives to be addressed. The reason is that, from a regional policy perspective, the smart specialisation approach offers a range of advantages for the design of appropriate innovation policy-making while allowing for the varied evolutionary nature of regional economies (McCann and Ortega-Argilés, 2015, 2–12).

There are several reasons smart specialisation is linked to the regional dimension. Todtling and Trippl (2005, 1204–1205) say that national and international technological and sectoral factors are essential; however, the regional dimension is of key importance, with increasing decentralisation and fragmentation of the state (Rončević and Tomšič, 2017, 13). To summarise several researchers[1]: (1) regions differ concerning their industrial specialisation pattern and their innovation performance (see Howells, 1999; Breschi, 2000; Paci and Usai, 2000: 2) it was shown that knowledge spillovers, which play a key role in the innovation process, are often spatially bounded (see Audretsch and Feldman, 1996; Anselin et al., 1997; Bottazzi and Peri, 2003: 3) the exchange of tacit knowledge for successful innovation requires intensive personal contacts of trust-based character which are facilitated by geographical proximity (see Polanyi, 1966; Maskell et al., 1998; Howells, 2002; Gertler, 2003; Morgan, 2004; e) policy competences and institutions are partly bound to subnational territories (see Cooke et al., 2000).

There is, however, a concern by McCann and Ortega-Argilés (2015, 4) that economic geography arguments suggest that the smart specialisation logic ought naturally to favour core regions at the expense of weaker regions, due to the lagging or peripheral regions often exhibit weaknesses in entrepreneurship and innovation due to a combination of reasons, which can be variously

1 For more on the topic, see also (Todtling and Trippl, 2005, 1204–1205).

sectoral, structural, transactional, technological, behavioural, related to resources and capabilities, related to risk and financial flows, related to externalities and issues of market failure, and also related to commercial and cultural perceptions (ibid). The EU official document 'Regional Policy Contributing to Smart Growth in Europe' (EC, 2012) steers the idea towards the need to identify sectors and technological domains on which regional policies should be tailored to promote local innovation processes in these specialisation fields (Camagni and Capello, 2013: 356). Also, we need to take into account an important objective of the European Union (EU) Cohesion Policy, known as RIS3 (Research and Innovation Strategies for Smart Specialisation) (see Foray, 2014, 1–101). The basic idea governing the generalised adoption of smart specialisation strategy within the framework of the Cohesion Policy was to effect a change of paradigm in the way in which these regional innovation policies were structured; the goal is now to encourage each region to identify transformation priorities that reflect and amplify existing local structures and competences, and thus produce original and unique competitive advantages (ibid.).

2. Issues of Regional Development

According to McCann and Ortega-Argilés (2015, 3), the original smart specialisation concept emerged from aspatial sectoral lines of thinking, but it increasingly shifted towards addressing regional growth issues as fundamental building blocks of national and European growth issues. To make the smart specialisation logic applicable to a regional context, the proponents of the concept interpreted the idea of a domain in terms of a region and applying the smart specialisation logic in this manner. McCann and Ortega-Argilés referred to David et al.. (2009), who argues that one of the features of many European regions is a weak correlation between the region's research and development (R&D) capabilities, its training specialisations, and its industrial structure. A regional policy recommendation from the smart specialisation proponents was, therefore, that rather than either pursuing 'one-size-fits-all' skills-training policies or always prioritising high-technology sectors over others, governments should foster human capital formation for the new 'knowledge needs' of the region's traditional industries which are starting to adapt and apply these new technologies. As such, this argument emphasises the critical role of knowledge diffusion processes between sectors, activities, and occupations, as well as explicitly avoiding automatically prioritising high-technology sectors by taking a broader systems perspective (McCann and Ortega-Argilés, 2015, 3).

Research on regional innovation has grown significantly over the past three decades, driven partly by advances in theoretical analysis, partly by the growing interest in innovation as a source of competitive advantage, and partly by the need for new policies to address regional inequalities and divergence (Asheim, Lawton Smith, and Oughton, 2011: 876; also Kleindienst, 2019; Fric, 2019). Much of the empirical work on regional systems have been based on well-functioning, successful regional economies and innovation in high-technology sectors (ibid: 880). However, there are many obstacles for peripheral regions, old industrial regions, and fragmented metropolitan regions (see Todtling and Trippl 2005, 1201–1216, see also Todtling, 1992; Cooke, 1995). As problem dimensions, one can list: (1) firms and regional clusters: cluster characteristics problems, innovation activities; (2) knowledge generation and diffusion: universities/research organisations, education, and training, knowledge transfer; (3) networks: network characteristic problems.

Further on, McCann and Ortega-Argilés say (2015, 4) that entrepreneurship tends to be lower in regions with lower population densities, lower in regions that are more sectorally specialised, lower in regions dominated by a small number of large firms, lower in regions with firms of limited international engagement, and lower in regions with low market potential (McCann and Ortega-Argilés, 2015, 4). The economic geography literature suggests that core regions offer greater potential rewards to the entrepreneurial search process in terms of the distribution, magnitude, and the learning capacity (McCann and Ortega-Argilés, 2015, 4). Other issues are also related to entrepreneurial skills (Ljubotina, 2019).

In contrast, looking through the prism of the Social-Fields-Approach (SOFIA), Rončević and Besednjak Valič (2019) discuss the role of regional development agencies for the implementation of regional development strategies (See also Rončević, 2012). In their perspective, they assert that RDAs can operate as actors in social fields connecting and bridging between global (mega) trends and local micro-contexts but also operate as an intermediary between stakeholders in the regional innovation system, shaped by the relevant social forces as outlined by the SOFIA (Rončević, 2012, 2020; Roncevic and Modic, 2011, 2012, 2018; Rončević et al., 2018; Rončević and Besednjak, 2019).

Todtling and Trippl (2005, 1204–1205) say that there is no one 'best practice' innovation policy approach that could be applied to any type of region,[2] but also there are some basic principles concerning innovation policy that are

2 See also Cooke et al. (2000), Isaksen (2001), and Nauwelaers and Wintjes (2003).

of relevance for all three types of regions (Todtling and Trippl, 2005, 1211–1215). There are also several types of RIS problems and failures, such as deficits concerning organisations and institutions and a lack of relations within and between the subsystems (Todtling and Trippl, 2005, 1205–1206, Cepoi, 2019; Cepoi and Golob, 2017; Besednjak Valič et al., 2020). Regions are often dealt with in an isolated manner, means that the interrelationships with other regions and with higher spatial levels (national, international) are left out of consideration (Todtling and Trippl, 2005, 1204).

To solve the obstacles, a snowball of questions emerges: what happens when we get foreign direct investments, funding opportunities, positive municipality policies (e.g., lower tax), new companies bringing high-tech knowledge, and new job opportunities? We need people to work there. People with the knowledge or who are willing and able to learn, are loyal productive workers. What if the region has a labour shortage? How does the region attract workers? Also, how does it retain workers? Furthermore, what do more people mean for the region? What about their culture, religion, language? Too often, the issues and obstacles are tackled one-sidedly. Research has been overly focused on specific details and not comprehending a broad picture in a cause-effect relationship with an interdisciplinary approach.

3. Development Prerequisites

At a theoretical level, research on regional innovation systems (RIS) has begun to model the innovation process in the context of a complex system (see Asheim, Lawton Smith and Oughton, 2011: 880). Knowledge is seen as central to this system, and the current literature has identified the importance of the geographical dimensions of knowledge transfer as a key variable shaping regional innovation performance. However, as Asheim, Lawton Smith and Oughton (ibid) state, many factors mediate this relationship: the strength of the science base and knowledge transfer system, the institutional setting; the financial system; education and training; the availability and mobility of skilled labor (human capital); and public policy measures designed to promote innovation and growth (ibid). Asheim, Lawton Smith, and Oughton (2011: 880) referring to Asheim and Gertler (ibid.), saying that the systems approach has begun to explore the inter-linkages between these different elements and how they combine to shape innovation and regional economic performance. The RIS approach has multiple theoretical antecedents drawing on the literature on Marshallian industrial districts, economic geography, innovative milieux, clusters, and national systems of innovation (ibid.)

4. Attracting and Attaining of Human Capital

Rodríguez-Pose and Vilalta-Bufı (2005: 545) claim that human capital has traditionally been regarded as one of the key factors behind economic growth. They claim that societies with a better endowment of human capital are considered to have a greater development potential than societies with scarce or inadequate human resources. Disparities in human capital endowment across nations, but especially across regions, are considerable and likely to affect the potential for convergence of those regions of the periphery of the European Union, where the greatest shortages in the human capital endowment are found (ibid). As we can read in Hansen and Niedomysl (2009, n.d.) Andersson (1985), Andersson and Stromquist (1988) and Glaeser (1994, 1998) (see Hansen and Niedomysl, 2009, n.d.), among others, that cities are increasingly becoming centres of economic activities in the knowledge economy. Romer (1986), Lucas (1988), and Glaeser (1994) (ibid.) argue that talented workers are closely linked to economic growth. The combination of the two is the departure of Florida (2002) who argues that the interplay between talented workers and cities are becoming the single most important element for regional competitiveness, because the more we move into a knowledge economy, the more important innovations become to maintain our current level of welfare as in the knowledge economy (ibid). To further the importance of human capital, Hansen and Niedomysl (2009, n.d.) say that a central element in contemporary regional development strategies is the ability for regions to attract and retain talented people. The underlying argument is that by attracting talented people, regions are better geared to meet the demand of competences of the knowledge economy and become more competitive (ibid). The academic literature (see Todtling and Trippl, 2005, 1203) states that knowledge, learning, and innovation are keys to economic development and competitiveness for firms, regions, and nations, but how is that reflected in attracting and attaining workers? Based on econometric analysis, Rodríguez-Pose and Vilalta-Bufı (2005: 560–561) assert that the in the case of European regions, factors such as the degree of job satisfaction, the balance between the skills on offer and those demanded, and the capacity to attract highly skilled migrants seem to have a higher sway over economic performance than the measures of human capital stock, traditionally used as proxies for human capital in most growth analyses. Their research results indicate that stock variables are more likely to be associated with wealth, whereas job satisfaction, matching indicators, and migration are more closely related to economic performance (Rodríguez-Pose and Vilalta-Bufı, 2005: 560–561). It is the case of the Danube region that is interesting in this aspect many less developed countries of eastern part of European Union face severe issues in de-population. For these countries, it is more a case of retaining the domestic educated population even before attracting foreign workers; re-industrialisation is seen as a potential mechanism to retain the domestic workforce (Besednjak Valič, 2019).

The 21st century economy increasingly revolves around knowledge or creative workers who are seen as a key sustainable competitive advantage (Thite, 2004). McCann and Ortega-Argilés (2015, 6) argue that the relationship between skills training and regional development depends on the links between the policy and changes in the local labour supply and how these changes dovetail with the local labour demand requirements; however, this raises a problem. Emphasising the regional embeddedness in the context of evolving global value chains may appear both to increase the vulnerability of the region to external shocks and to reduce the possibilities for knowledge spillovers, precisely because it implies increasing the specialisation of the region. Therefore, to counter these problems, it is necessary to develop a strategy to allow the less prosperous regions to diversify not to specialise (ibid., also Rončević et al., 2010). Asheim, Lawton Smith, and Oughton (2011: 886) argue that the question of how labour markets and human capital operate within RIS is under-theorised. In particular, there is a need to integrate analysis of the generation and employment of human capital and talent within regions (including labour migration) and the role that human capital plays in shaping absorptive capacity and innovation performance (ibid).

Increased education levels and intensified residential mobility among the highly educated have expanded the importance of human capital mobility in contemporary societies (Butler and Hamnett, 2007). The high residential mobility of young university and college graduates has been shown to be crucial for the process of human and financial capital redistribution (e.g., Faggian and McCann, 2009). Spatial mobility among the highly skilled is particularly directed towards urban regions functioning as economic and social attraction pools and offering affordable rental housing (see Florida, 2002; Whisler, Waldorf, Mulligan and Plane, 2008; Venhorst, Van Dijk and Van Wissen, 2011; Golob and Makarovič, 2018). Understanding the factors that attract people to move to different places is pivotal for scholars of regional science and has consequently stimulated a great deal of debate and empirical studies. An important issue has been whether employment opportunities or amenities are decisive when migrants make their decisions about where to move (e.g. Millington, 2000; Glaeser et al., 2001; Gottlieb, 2003; Adamson et al., 2004; Niedomysl, 2005; Gottlieb and Joseph, 2006; Ferguson et al., 2007; Chen and Rosenthal, 2008; Houston et al., 2008; Whisler et al., 2008; Scott, 2010; Niedomysl and Hansen, 2010; Golob, 2009; Golob, 2014).

Acquaintance with or knowledge about the available housing stock, availability of childcare and primary schools, cultural amenities, language or regional boundaries, social networks, and perceived environmental quality constitute location-specific factors of future research interest (Imeraj et al., 2017). Several studies have shown that artistic/cultural, and technology/innovation communities that constitute a cultural economy are best able to attract talent and boost urban growth (Stolarick and Florida, 2006 in Thite, 2011; Wojan, Lambert, and McGranahan, 2007 in Thite, 2011). Location-specific amenities offered in urban contexts include natural amenities (Graves, 1980), man-made amenities (Blomquist, Berger and Hoehn, 1988), and social, cultural, and skill-dependent amenities (Florida, 2002). Conditional on the extent to which different amenities are satisfactory, people are more or less likely to prefer a particular destination (Whisler et al., 2008). Given that psychological costs of migration are reduced through knowledge of local facilities, the proximity of relatives and availability of information (Coniglio and Prota, 2008; Delisle and Shearmur, 2010), the regional familiarity with the former location of the HEI could matter significantly to graduates' propensity to settle in the city of HE after getting a degree. Hence, 'location-specific capital' (Davanzo, 1983, p. 553), built up as social networks and knowledge of local facilities and amenities through residential experience during HE study, eases the move (Venhorst, 2013; Imeraj et al., 2017). Imeraj et al. (2017) add that location-specific advantages appear likely to become less useful once graduates have built up economic capital through the expansion of a professional career and an increased wage. Importantly, the earnings of graduates at the start of their professional careers are lower than later on, and so are their tax contributions.

Furthermore, the replenishment with non-local graduates (for example, the exchange of graduates between HEI locations in Belgium) is negligible. In line with the importance of regional familiarity for graduate residential choices (Venhorst, 2013 in Imeraj et al., 2017), non-locally produced graduates tend to settle in the close environment of their former HEI or their family but rarely in another HE city (ibid). However, Niedomysl and Hansen (2010, n.d.) argue that the evidence they gathered suggests that amenities should be considered as preferences, not needs or demands, which makes amenities relevant mainly when other factors, such as jobs and affordable housing, can be fulfilled at two potential destinations. It is, therefore, debatable whether amenities should be given a prominent position in the literature on the geography of talent until their importance has been empirically and theoretically justified (ibid). They continue by stating that their findings suggest that outdoor activities and recreation are valued highly by the migrants. This factor appears particularly important for the elderly and people with high incomes. Authors then refer to Andersen, Hansen, and Niedomysl, (2009) (ibid). saying that it is known that amenities that are highly valued change character over the life course. When people are young, urban life is important, but getting older and getting settled with family and children, and similar, cause changes in people's location preferences. This is an important notion because it puts planners in a dilemma. Young people, whose migration propensities are high, are the most mobile; they are attracted by cultural and entertainment facilities (ibid). Nevertheless, as Wolfe et al. (2005 in Asheim, Lawton Smith and Oughton 2011: 886) state, the possibility of talented people being attracted, trained and retained in particular locations depends on the quality of the labour market as well as the characteristics of places, institutions, and policy (ibid.). Consequently, the evolution of a localised expert labour market system involves a complex interaction of technical, economic, social, and political forces, which collectively determine how economies function (Wilkinson, 1983).

Also, we need to consider that some types of knowledge (Markusen 1996 in Asheim, Lawton Smith and Oughton, 2011: 883) see and intellectual capital are less mobile than other resources and because the complexity of transferring knowledge from its basic form into new product and process innovations, and the diffusion of innovations, is a complex, dynamic process that is difficult to replicate and transfer across borders. As a result, even in the face of globalisation, localities and regions may grow in importance as the increasing role of intellectual capital leads to the creation of what Markusen (ibid) has termed 'sticky places in slippery space'. Asheim, Lawton Smith, and Oughton (2011: 883) argue that this can be contrasted to the branch plant era in which the emphasis was on productivity rather than innovation and the R&D activities of many of the major foreign-owned companies were located outside the region. Coupled with a strategy based on attracting (footloose) inward investment, the regional policy also centred on entrepreneurship and the creation of small firms, but the strategy failed to ensure that the necessary skill base was created in the labour force and it failed to bring about significant regional development (ibid).

Thite (2011, n.d.) asserts that some of the off-the-job factors that are considered under the model such as 'links' with schools and membership in sports/social/religious associations, 'fit' with type and size of the location, its climate, amenities, and activities, are the reasons why employees stay with their employer despite being unhappy with their employment. Other non-job-related reasons such as families' inability or reluctance to move to another location (ibid) also play the role. Thus social ties are also important. Winther and Hansen

(2006) found that, at least in the outer-city areas of Copenhagen, Denmark, social relations play an important role for the location of economic activities of people who tend to locate their businesses close to their homeland home is often chosen based on relatives and close friends. (ibid). Reflecting the idea of people's being 'situated or connected in a social web', embeddedness has several key aspects: the extent to which people have 'links' to other people or activities, the extent to which their jobs and communities 'fit' other aspects in their 'life spaces', and the ease with which links could be broken, that is, what they would give up or 'sacrifice' if they left their present settings (Mitchell et al., 2001; Lee et al., 2004). Social ties and relations can significantly influence the realisation of human dignity, which is important both from individual as well as social perspectives (Kleindienst, 2017; Kleindienst and Tomšič, 2017; Kleindienst and Tomšič, 2018; Kleindienst, 2019).

According to Henry and Pinch (2000 in Asheim, Lawton Smith and Oughton 2011: 886) 'place' can be a powerful attractor (and creator) of highly skilled labour, and that critical mass is necessary to attract creative workers to a locality (ibid.). Fritsch and Slavtchev (Asheim, Lawton Smith and Oughton, 2011, 800) find that population density has a positive effect on RIS efficiency, indicating that R&D activity is more productive in agglomerations than in rural areas. Also, there is evidence of spillover effects within the private sector and between public research institutes (universities, Max-Planck and Fraunhofer) and the private sector (ibid.).

Some research does not support the above findings. In the research in Germany, Buch et al. (2017). discovered that the results somewhat differ for overall migration and moves that also involve a change of the workplace. Labour market conditions are more important than amenities if migration comes along with a change of workplace (ibid.). The research was done based on amenities, such as the robust effects of sunshine duration, the share of restaurant workers, and above-average cultural diversity. Head and Lloyd-Ellis (2012, 1586) state that in a version of the economy with both high unemployment (due to lower rates of hiring) and high mobility, the effect of ownership on aggregate unemployment can be large (as illustrated by our high unemployment calibration). Such a configuration of parameters appears, however, to be counterfactual: countries that have high rates of mobility tend to have low average unemployment (e.g., the U.S.), and countries with low rates of mobility tend to have relatively high rates of average unemployment (e.g., continental Europe). We do, however, need to stress that their finding was based on lower rates of hiring, meaning when jobs are scarce, and one is willing and/or able to migrate for work. As written, the findings are quite local-focused but, nevertheless, have to be taken into consideration.

5. Where to Go from Here?

The competitiveness of cities has received growing attention for regional development policies and planning during recent decades because urban areas are increasingly becoming centres of economic activity in the knowledge-based economies of highly developed countries (Hansen and Niedomysl, 2009). Moreover, human capital is increasingly considered to be a crucial resource for knowledge-intensive production and, thus, for the competitiveness of cities. In contrast to other factors of production, highly skilled workers are highly mobile. Therefore, regions need to provide favourable living and working conditions to attract and retain highly skilled labour (Buch et al., 2017).

Kanter (in Thite, 2011) says that to survive in the new environment, communities need both 'magnets' and 'glue'. LaFaive and Weislak add (2003 in Thite, 2011) that *magnets* refer to the factors that attract a flow of external resources such as new companies and new people to renew and expand skills and contribute to the economic health of the region. *Magnet factors* refer to a healthy and well-educated workforce, a clean environment, a vibrant business climate, and a solid social and cultural infrastructure. However, communities also need 'glue' in a form of the physical infrastructure that supports daily life and work, social infrastructure to solve problems and promote the economic and social well-being of all their members (ibid.).

So, what attracts people to a place? Based on literature, Donald (2001) identified eight quality of life indicators:

- Social cohesion, indicated by participation, inclusion, belonging, recognition and legitimacy,
- Human services, including quality and accessibility of healthcare, community support services, and social safety net,
- Learning, including education and skill levels, quality of public education and quality of public research institutions,
- Community safety, indicated by levels of crime,
- Affordable housing, availability, and accessibility,
- Public transportation, availability, and accessibility,
- Environmental quality,
- Culture, recreation, and lifestyle amenities (ibid.).

Studying the existing literature, we have also identified the importance of life periods, indicating that it is relevant at which stage of one's life one currently is, which are strongly linked to the age of a person. We identified four life periods, that affect the decision of residence:

- 'Deciding for study' period
- 'Finishing studies at HEI' period
- 'Have some money' period
- 'After retirement/elderly' period.

Since the majority of research deals with highly skilled people, the above periods are set only for them. But what about the 'regular' workers? One could argue that they could have different life quality indicators (e.g., they appreciate affordable housing; in contrast, highly skilled workers with high income appreciate more exclusive housing). Also, they do not attend HEI, meaning they do not share the first two periods of skilled people. Generally, one can argue that it is not important only to understand what attracts and attains people but also determine what kind of workers you would like to attract so stakeholders can focus the investments and market the location. In the global war for talent (see Victoria 2010 in Thite, 2011), enterprises face a stark choice: create a brand or get branded. Melbourne and Victoria in Australia, for instance, are using Brand Victoria and 'Victoria – The Place to Be', which are destination-marketing tools that aim to build a strong and meaningful identity for Melbourne and Victoria by positioning the state as a destination of choice for international students, investors, skilled migrants, and tourists. It is a creative solution and brand strategy that provides common brand values, key messages, and a unique brand mark and visual identity (ibid).

Considering the Donald indicators (Donald, 2011) and life periods we indicated above and the level of workers' skills, an overview of how to attract and attain people can become quite complicated. Who is our target group? Highly skilled or 'regular' blue collar workers? The second group is larger in number and are not interested in cultural events? A model that would help answer these questions and shape the marketing approach to attracting and attaining people would be most helpful for the all included actors that shape the triple helix – HEI, local and/or regional decision-makers and businesses. To do that, we need additional information from various regions. Based on the literature review (see Jean Monnet Centre of Excellence TIR 2020 project[3]), a research

3 Jean Monnet Center of Excellence, Technology and Innovations in Regional Development for Europe 2020 (TIR2020), Co-funded by the Erasmus+ programme

toolkit was prepared, covering the open questions on technologies, innovation, and regional policy to implement extensive research among 20 countries in Europe. Among 20 thematic slots,[4] there are also two covering the attracting and attaining workers:

1. *Does your region have the capacity to attract talented people?* Examples of important aspects concerning capacity to attract talented people within the region: Professional Development, Rewards, and Recognition, Migration Policy, Integration, etc. Additional Questions:
   (a) Which are the mechanisms through which the region attracts talented people?
   (b) How can these mechanisms be improved?
   (c) Who are the actors that contribute to attracting talented people in the region?[5]
2. *Does your region have the capacity to retain talented people?* Examples of important aspects concerning capacity to retain talented people within the region: Professional Development, Rewards, and Recognition, Migration Policy, Integration, etc. Additional Questions
   (a) Which are the mechanisms through which the region retains talented people?
   (b) How can these mechanisms be improved?

---

of the European Union, Key Action: Cooperation for innovation and the exchange of good practices, Action Type: Knowledge Alliances for higher education, Project Reference: 587540-EPP-1-2017-1-SI-EPPJMO-CoE.

4 1. Innovation level, 2. Information Circulation, 3. Enterprises' R&D involvement, 4. Open Innovation, 5. Institutional Support for Innovation, 6. Attract talented people, 7. Retain talented people, 8. Innovation policy, 9. Network Contribution, 10. Cooperation between regional stakeholders, 11. Cooperation with outsiders, 12. Trust, 13. Entrepreneurship and Creativity 14. Learning framework, 15. Competition (Perception), 16. Globalization, 17. Transnational Value Chain Embeddedness, 18. Region TIER, 19. Role of TVC for R&D, 20. Regional Economic dependence for TVC and TR.

5 Labels are:
1. The region cannot attract people, even for less demanding non-creative jobs.
2. The region attracts some people, but mostly for less creative jobs.
3. The region is relatively successful in attracting people including more creative jobs.
4. The region is very successful and is able to attract the most talented people required in creative jobs.

(c) Who are the actors that contribute to retaining talented people in the region?[6]

Despite the many challenges to comparative research (Rončević et al., 2017), the goal of future research is to get information on a broad scale of Europe. The data obtained could be later on combined with the statistical information on different indicators, such as BDP per capita, innovation, workers' added value, average income, real-estate ownership, education levels, infrastructure development, life satisfaction, culture indicators, health indicators, etc. Based on selected indicators an in-depth analysis would be possible in aim to detect good practices in attracting and attaining workers.

References

Adam, F., Makarovič, M., Rončević, B., and Tomšič, M. (2005). *The Challenges of Sustained Development: The Role of Socio-cultural Factors in East-Central Europe*. New York; Budapest: Central European University Press.

Adamson, D. W., Clark, D. E., and Partridge, M. D. (2004). *Do urban agglomeration effects and household amenities have a skill bias?* Journal of Regional Science, 44 (2), 201–223.

Anselin, L., Varga, A., and Acs, Z. (1997). *Local geographic spillovers between university research and high technology innovations*. Journal of Urban Economics 42 (3), 422–448.

Asheim, Bjorn T., Lawton Smith H., and Oughton C. (2011). *Regional innovation systems: Theory, empirics and policy*. Regional Studies, 45 (7), 875–889.

Audretsch, D., and Feldman, M. (1996). *Innovative clusters and the industry life cycle*. Review of Industrial Organisation, 11 (2), 253–273.

Besednjak Valič, T. (2019). Innovation, Digitalisation, and the HPC in the Danube Region. In Rončević, B., Coscodaru, R., Fric, U. (eds.). *Go with the Flow: High Performance Computing and Innovations in the Danube Region*. London; Budapest; Ljubljana: Vega Press.

---

6 Labels are:

1. The region has no capacity to retain people, even those required for less creative and manual jobs.
2. The region is able to retain people, but mostly in less creative jobs.
3. The region is relatively successful in retaining people, including those required for more creative jobs.
4. The region is very successful in retaining the most talented people required for creative jobs.

Besednjak Valič, T., Kolar, J., and Lamut, U. (2020). *Three scenarios of innovation and technology transfer: The case of key enabling technologies in the Danube Region*. Journal of Engineering and Applied Sciences, 15, 3619–3623.

Blomquist, G. C., Berger, M. C., and Hoehn, J. P. (1988). *New estimates of quality of life in urban areas*. American Economic Review, 78, 89–107.

Bottazzi, L., and Peri, G. (2003). *Innovation and spillovers in regions: Evidence from European patent data*. European Economic Review, 4 (4), 687–710.

Breschi, S. (2000). *The geography of innovation: A cross-industry analysis*. Regional Studies, 34, 213–229.

Buch, T., Hamann, S., Niebuhr, A., and Rossen, A. (2017). *How to woo the smart ones? Evaluating the determinants that particularly attract highly qualified people to cities*. Journal of Urban Affairs, 39 (6), 764–782.

Butler, T., and Hamnett, C. (2007). *The geography of education: Introduction*. Urban Studies, 44 (7), 1161–1174.

Camagni, R., and Capello, R. (2013). *Regional innovation patterns and the EU regional policy reform: Toward smart innovation policies*. Growth and Change, 44 (2), 355–389.

Cepoi, V., and Golob, T. (2017). *Innovation performance in the EU comparative perspective: The interplay of social forces in the context of national innovation systems*. Comparative Sociology 16 (4), 555–579.

Chen, Y., and Rosenthal, S. (2008). *Local amenities and life-cycle migration: Do people move for jobs or fun?* Journal of Urban Economics, 64, 519–537.

Coniglio, N. D., and Prota, F. (2008). *Human capital accumulation and migration in a peripheral EU region: The case of Basilicata*. Papers in Regional Science, 87, 77–95.

Cooke, P. (ed.), (1995). *The Rise of the Rustbelt*. London: UCL Press.

Cooke, P., Boekholt, P., and Todtling, F. (2000). *The Governance of Innovation in Europe*. London: Pinter.

Davanzo, J. (1983). *Repeat migration in the United States: Who moves back and who moves on?* Review of Economics and Statistics, 65, 552–559.

Delisle, F., and Shearmur, R. (2010). *Where does all the talent flow? Migration of young graduates and nongraduates, Canada 1996–2001*. Canadian Geographer/Le Géographe Canadien, 54, 305–323.

Donald, B. (2001). *Economic competitiveness and quality of life in city regions: Compatible concepts?* Canadian Journal of Urban Research 10 (2), 259–274.

European Commission (2012). *Revision of the state aid rules for research and development and innovation, Issues paper*. Brussels: Competition

Directorate-Geneneral for Competition, https://ec.europa.eu/competition/state_aid/legislation/rdi_issues_paper.pdf, accessed February 2020.

Faggian A., and McCann, P. (2009). *Universities, agglomerations and graduate human capital mobility.* Tijdschrift voor Economische en Sociale Geografie 100 (2), 210–223.

Ferguson, M., Ali, K., Olfert, R. M., and Partridge, M. (2007). *Voting with their feet: Jobs versus amenities.* Growth and Change, 38 (1), 77–110.

Florida, R. (2002). *The Rise of the Creative Class.* New York: Basic Books.

Foray, D. (ed.). (2014). *Smart Specialisation: Opportunities and Challenges for Regional Innovation Policy.* Regional Studies Association. The Global Forum for City and Regional Research, Development and Policy. Routledge; Tailor and Francis Group.

Fric, U. (2019). *Impact of circular economy as the EU's ambitious policy.* Research in Social Change, 11(2), 79–96. DOI:10.2478/rsc-2019-0010.

Gertler, M. (2003). *Tacit knowledge and the economic geography of context or the undefinable tacitness of being (there).* Journal of Economic Geography, 3(1), 75–99.

Glaeser, E. L., Kolko J., and Saiz, A. (2001). *Consumer city.* Journal of Economic Geography, 1 (1), 27–50.

Golob, Tea, (2009). *Slovenian migrants in transnational social spaces: Exploring multilayered identifications and ambivalent belongings*, Anthropological notebooks, 15 (3), 65–77.

Golob, Tea, (2014). *Exploring identifications in the transnational social sphere: The potential of social fields*, Sociologija i prostor: časopis za istraživanje prostornog i sociokulturnog razvoja, 52 (2) (199), 123–140.

Golob, Tea, and Matej Makarovič, (2018). *Student mobility and transnational social ties as factors of reflexivity*, Social Sciences, 7 (3), 1–18.

Gottlieb, P. D. (2003). *Economy versus lifestyle in the inter-metropolitan migration of the young: A preliminary look at the 2000 Census.* International Journal of Economic Development 5 (3).

Gottlieb, P. D., and Joseph, G. (2006). *College-to-work migration of technology graduates and holders of doctorates within the United State.* Journal of Regional Science, 46 (4), 627–659.

Graves, P. (1980). *Migration and climate.* Journal of Regional Science, 20 (2), 227–237.

Hansen, H. K., and Niedomysl, T. (2009). *Migration of the creative class: Evidence from Sweden.* Journal of Economic Geography, 9(2), 191–206.

Head, A., and Lloyd-Ellis, H. (2012). *Housing liquidity, mobility, and the labour market.* The Review of Economic Studies, 79 (4), 1559–1589.

Houston, D., Findlay, A., Harrison R., and Mason C. (2008). *Will attracting the 'creative class' boost economic growth in old industrial regions? A case study of Scotland.* Geografiska Annaler, Series B: Human Geography, 90 (2), 133–149.

Howells, J. (1999). Regional systems of innovation? In: Archibugi, D., Howells, J., Michie, J. (eds.), *Innovation Policy in a Global Economy.* Cambridge: Cambridge University Press, pp. 67–93.

Howells, J. (2002). *Tacit knowledge, innovation and economic geography.* Urban Studies, 39 (5–6), 871–884.

Imeraj, L., Willaert, D., Finney, N., and Gadeyne, S. (2017). *Cities' attraction and retention of graduates: A more-than-economic approach.* Regional Studies, 52 (8), 1086–1097.

Isaksen, A. (2001). *Building regional innovation systems: Is endogenous industrial development possible in the global economy?* Canadian Journal of Regional Science, 1, 101–120.

Kleindienst, P. (2017). *Understanding the different dimensions of human dignity: Analysis of the decision of the constitutional court of the Republic of Slovenia on the "Tito Street" Case*', DANUBE: Law and Economics Review, 8/3, 117–137. DOI: 10.1515/danb-2017-0009.

Kleindienst, P. (2019a). *Zgodovinski temelji sodobne paradigme človekovega dostojanstva*, Phainomen*a* 28/108–109, 259–282. DOI: 10.32022/PHI28.2019.108-109.11.

Kleindienst, P. (2019b). *Economic and social security in EU: Reforming Slovenian law on social entrepreneurship.* Research in Social Change, 11(2), 14–34. DOI:10.2478/rsc-2019-0007.

Kleindienst, P., and Tomšič, M. (2017). *Human dignity as the foundation of democratic political culture: Legal and philosophical perspective.* Law, Culture and the Humanities, 1–20. DOI: 10.177/143872117738229.

Kleindienst, P., and Tomšič, M. (2018). *C̆lovekovo dostojanstvo kot del politične kulture v novih demokracijah: postkomunistična Slovenija.* Bogoslovni vestnik, 78(1), 159–172.

Ljubotina, P. (2020). *The influence of entrepreneurial skills, educationa and risk perception on career choice intent: The case of european students with family business background.* Research in Social Change, 12(3), 23–37. DOI: 10.2478/rsc-2020-0002.

Makarovič, M., Šušteršič, J., and Rončević, B. (2014). *Is Europe 2020 set to fail?: The cultural political economy of the EU grand strategies.* European Planning Studies, 22(3), 610–626.

Maskell, P., Eskelinen, H., Hannibalsson, I., Malmberg, A., and Vatne, E. (1998). *Competitiveness, localised learning and regional development. Specialisation and prosperity in small open economies*. London: Routledge.

McCann, P., and Ortega-Argilés, R. (2015). *Smart specialization, regional growth and applications to European Union cohesion policy.* Regional Studies, 49 (8), 1–101.

Millington J. (2000). *Migration and age: The effect of age on sensitivity to migration stimuli*. Regional Studies, 34 (6), 521–533.

Mitchell, T. R., Holtom, B. C., Lee, T. W., Sablynski, C. J., and Erez, M. (2001). *Why people stay: Using job embeddedness to predict voluntary turnover.* Academy of Management Journal, 44 (6), 1102–21.

Modic, D., and Rončević, B. (2018). *Social topography for sustainable innovation policy: Putting institutions, social networks and cognitive frames in their place*. Comparative sociology, 17(1), 100–127.

Morgan, K. (2004). *The exaggerated death of geography: Learning, proximity and territorial innovation systems.* Journal of Economic Geography, 4, 3–21.

Nauwelaers, C., and Wintjes, R. (2003). Towards a new paradigm for innovation policy? In: Asheim, B., Isaksen, A., Nauwelaers, C., Todtling, F. (eds.), *Regional Innovation Policy for Small-Medium Enterprises*. Cheltenham: Edward Elgar, pp. 193–220.

Niedomysl, T. (2005). *Tourism and interregional migration in Sweden: an explorative approach.* Population, Space and Place, 11 (5), 187–204, <https://doi.org/10.1068/a39177>, accessed February 2020.

Niedomysl, T., and Hansen, H. K. (2010). *What matters more for the decision to move: Jobs versus Amenities.* Environment and Planning A, 42 (7), 1636–1649.

Paci, R., and Usai, S. (2000). *Technological enclaves and industrial districts: An analysis of the regional distribution of innovative activity in Europe*. Regional Studies, 34 (2), 97–114.

Polanyi, M. (1966). *The Tacit Dimension*. London: Routledge.

Rodríguez-Pose, A., and Vilalta-Bufi, M. (2005). *Education, migration, and job satisfaction: The regional returns of human capital in the EU.* Journal of Economic Geography, 5(5), 545–566.

Rončević, B. (2012). Regional development agencies and changing social fields: Towards a sociology of regional systems of innovation. In: Bellini, N., Danson, M., and Halkier, H. (eds.) *Regional Development Agencies: The Next Generation?: Networking, Knowledge and Regional Policies*. London; New York: Routledge, 87–101.

Rončević, B. (2020). *Technology and innovations in regional development for Europe 2020: Jean Monnet Centre of Excellence TIR 2020 for smart, inclusive and sustainable growth*. Research in Social Change, 12(3), 5–14. DOI:10.2478/rsc-2020-0011.

Rončević, B., and Besednjak Valič, T. (2019). *How to think about regional development agencies as a sociologist*. The Social Sciences, 14(9), 326–334.

Rončević, B., Makarovič, M., Tomšič, M., and Cepoi, V. (2018). Methodological solutions for comparative research on transformations. In: Vihalemm, P., Masso, A., and Opermann, S. (eds.) *The Routledge International Handbook of European Social Transformations*. London and New York: Routledge, 57–70.

Rončević, B., and Modic, D. (2011). *Regional systems of innovations as social fields*. Sociologija i prostor: časopis za istraživanje prostornoga i sociokulturnog razvoja, 49(191), 313–333.

Rončević, B., and Modic, D. (2012). Social fields of technological innovations. In: Genov, N. (ed.) *Global Trends and Regional Development*. New York: Routledge, 226–247.

Rončević, Borut, Šušteršič, J., Wostner, P., and Besednjak Valič, T. (2010). *Quo Vadis, Slovenia? Between framework conditions and internal capabilities*. Managing Global Transitions, 8(4), 353–380.

Rončević, B., and Tomšič, M. (2017). Perspectives of information society: Bricolage of manifestations. In: Rončević, B. and Tomšič, M. (eds.) *Information Society and Its Manifestations: Economy, Politics, Culture*. Frankfurt am Main: Peter Lang, 9–21.

Scott, A. J. (2010). *Jobs or amenities? Destination choices of migrant engineers in the USA*. Papers in Regional Science, 89 (1), 43–63.

Thite, M. (2004). *Managing People in the New Economy*. New Delhi: Response (Sage).

Thite, M. (2011). *Smart cities: Implications of urban planning for human resource development*. Human Resource Development International, 14 (5), 623–631.

Todtling, F. (1992). *Technological change at the regional level: The role of location, firm structure, and strategy*. Environment and Planning, 24 (11), 1565–1584.

Todtling, F., and Trippl, M. (2005). *One size fits all? Towards a differentiated regional innovation policy approach*. Elsevier, Research Policy, 34 (8), 1203–1219.

Venhorst, V. (2013). *Graduate migration and regional familiarity*. Tijdschrift voor Economische en Sociale Geografie, 104 (1), 109–119.

Venhorst, V., Van Dijk, J., and Van Wissen, L. (2011). *An analysis of trends in spatial mobility of Dutch graduates*. Spatial Economic Analysis, 6 (1), 57–82.

Whisler, R. L., Waldorf, B. S., Mulligan, G. F., and Plane, D. A. (2008). *Quality of life and the migration of the college-educated: A life-course approach.* Growth and Change, 39, 58–94.

Wilkinson, F. (1983). *Productive systems.* Cambridge Journal of Economics, 7 (3–4), 413–429.

Winther, L., and Hansen, H. K. (2006). *The economic geographies of the outer city: Industrial dynamics and imaginary spaces of location in Copenhagen.* European Planning Studies, 14, 1387–1406.

Victor Cepoi

Innovation Process in the Framework of Social-Fields-Approach (SOFIA): A Qualitative Assessment for Ireland and Slovenia

Abstract: Relying on the Social-Fields-Approach (SOFIA), the analysis considers institutions, networks, and cognitive frames as an alternative explanation for innovation processes by encompassing the aspects of different social fields on the regional level. As case studies, we selected the regions of South-East Ireland and South-East Slovenia, which have different levels of innovation performance. The analysis of the semi-structured interviews emphasised the role of social forces. As a result, these constitute special components for explaining innovation processes in the selected case studies. Nonetheless, the results offer insights for regional mechanisms within the innovation performance, focusing on an approach toward innovation beyond simple macro-economic indicators.

1. Introduction

The development of modern economies is complex (Adam et al., 2005) and bound to innovation processes. These processes, linked to knowledge and information, are important for companies, which are considered the drivers of economic change, enabling them to attract and retain their competitive advantage (Nowacki and Bachnik, 2016: 1577; Pandiloska Jurak, 2020). The complexity of the political, social, and economic environments determines the way different stakeholders interact. Even more, it not only influences society's daily interactions but also how technological transformations happen. Understanding technological transformation is key moment to approaching to technological progress and its effects on regional development, especially in cases in which mainstream economic approaches are no longer able to explain all the changes that are happening.

Current economic realities determine the need for less developed regions to catch up, and innovation processes can be regarded as a solution. Countries and regions need to be constantly innovative. It is of upmost importance to understand what the determinants of innovation processes are. Thus, it is very difficult to explain new economic realities with the help of mainstream economic approaches. In the business world (see Pandiloska Jurak and Pinterič, 2012; Besednjak Valič et al., 2020) and the public sector, various models and standards based on specific criteria and methodological tools measure and value quality, effectiveness, efficiency, and excellence. However, it is necessary to pay special attention to the selection of a model, which assesses the complexity (ibid.). The goal is to have a broader explanation model for innovation processes, which consider not only the economic factors but also reflect other factors that influence the process of innovation (Rončević and Besednjak Valič, 2019; Rončević et al., 2010).

The research aims to test a robust tool that will allow stakeholders not only to see the strengths and weaknesses of the region, but also to acknowledge which aspects of the innovation process have to be considered. Thus, the innovative aspect of the approach is based on the theoretical framework of Social Fields. It emphasises the importance of innovation of three social forces, which are in a relationship of reciprocal influence: institutions, networks and cognitive frames (Beckert, 2010).

2. Social-Fields-Approach (SOFIA)

It is important to regard innovation processes operating in a given market, thus determining the operational aspect of any innovation process. Even more, the market must be perceived as politically and socially constructed. As Fligstein (2001) argues, the social construction reflects two aspects, governments' interventions and a country's culture and history of class relations. The capitalist national system is understood as a whole, thus links it to state involvement and ownership in key industries, capital allocations, labour relations, tax systems or even culture. All these aspects are considered under the Social Fields theory and acknowledge the interactions on different levels (Fligstein and McAdam, 2012). As the authors point out, the interaction milieu between different actors and social environments are considered as social arenas or local orders. It determines to look at states, regions or any environment are as a complex system of fields. Within these social orders, actors gather and frame their actions vis-à-vis one another (Fligstein, 2001: 108). The actors' actions and interactions depend on the social structures and individual actions. As Beckert (2010) emphasises, the theory of Social Fields has at its forefront three social forces: institutions, social networks, and cognitive frames. These social forces are relevant for the economic outcome, thus, innovation in our case.

Additionally, these three social forces are in a relationship of reciprocal influence. As Beckert (2010: 605) indicates, institutions influence the structure of social networks, while networks establish power to shape institutions. For cognitive frames, institutions make certain cultural meanings socially relevant, whereas cognitive frames shape perceptions of institutions. Lastly, social networks shape and diffuse cognitive frames, while cognitive frames shape perceptions of network structures. On the basis of these premises, the Social-Fields-Approach (SOFIA) to study the social underpinnings of innovations started to develop more than a decade ago (Rončević, 2012, 2020; Roncevic and Modic, 2011, 2012, 2018; Rončević and Besednjak, 2019; Roncevic et al., 2018; Cepoi and Golob, 2017).

2.1. Institutions

This particular social force influences the way regional development and innovation processes occurs within a particular region or country. Thus, speaking about institutions, we refer to '... set of rules, compliance procedures, and moral and ethical behavioural norms designed to constrain the behaviour of individuals in the interests of maximizing the wealth or utility of principals' (North 1981). One can indicate the political-administrative regulations or, more specifically, provisions and laws (Jakobsen and Aarset, 2010). As a result, the behaviour of different economic actors and citizens (Tomšič and Kleindienst, 2017; Golob and Makarovič, 2017) is determined by this regulatory framework. As the authors indicate, the regulatory framework can have both positive and negative stimuli. For example, an institution can protect companies from costly and high-risk innovative processes, especially in their first period. It also refers to research and development activities, by stimulating companies to make investments and promote innovation processes (Jakobsen and Aarset, 2010, 930). Simultaneously, the innovation process can be hindered in a particular milieu by the restrictive origin of these regulations. It will determine the market to influence the competition. It will be burdened by limiting fair competition. Companies will have to re-adjust their strategies, including the research and development process. However, if these institutions provide necessary regulatory framework (see also Fric, 2019; Rončević, 2019; Pandiloska Jurak, 2020) for a fair competition in a given milieu, innovations and all processes related to them will thrive (Jakobsen and Aarset, 2010: 929).

2.2. Social Networks

Another social force that has to be considered in explaining any economic interactions are the social networks. Some are even talking about the process of 'networkisation' in the information society (Rončević and Tomšič, 2017). It influences the process of development in various ways. The interconnectedness of technologies and actors, the adaption of a certain innovative practice or innovation itself, and its adoption are influenced by other actors, who influence each other's behaviour. Additionally, the adoption of a new product or practice depends on the conviction that other actors will do it (Aarikka-Stenroos et al., 2014: 366). R&D and aspects of commercialisation rely on network actors.

It is argued that knowledge in new economic realities can be measured by looking at the share of knowledge-intensive industries and income distribution in the world (Ahrweiler and Keane, 2013). The realisation of norms, ideas, and innovation becomes a reality with the help of social networks. Because social networks perceive individuals within their social context and acknowledge the influence of relationships with others on one's behaviour, the latter can promote innovation processes (Kolleck, 2013). Moreover, social networks can expand learning opportunities. An innovation is accepted when it is supported by interconnected actors. When they gain individual support, the chances of being accepted drop considerably. Thus, we can say that social networks have the role of fostering change and promoting the diffusion of innovation processes (Kolleck, 2013: 2). Strategic networks rely on joint marketing and production activities, but the geographic area where firms are part of the innovation process is also important.

Moreover, the interactions between them are based on reciprocity and trust, which are encouraged through a shared interest to carry out innovation. The aim is to increase competitiveness not only for firms, but also the region (Thorgren et al., 2009: 153). At the same time, it must be understood that strategic networks differ from alliances, which are characterised by a high number of member firms, each engaging in different activities based on the level of the interest. As a result, it can be said that these networks lose some of their cooperative form (Fukugawa, 2006). As Fukugawa highlights, some members focus on joint innovation projects, while others focus on information acquisition. Firms keep a certain degree of independence even though cooperation requires exchanging resources, ideas, or knowledge (Rosenfeld, 1996). Strategic networks are a distinct form of cooperation, which is flexible in within-network constellations, though not losing of its strong overarching influence (Thorgren et al., 2009: 153).

3.3. Cognitive Frames

Finally, the last social force that Beckert talks about are the cognitive frames. The literature points that the role of culture can hinder or positively influence the innovation process, though many details about the conditions under which these processes happen, remain under-researched DiMaggio (1997: 268). As the author indicates, on the one had cultural elements help in pursuing the valued end. On the other, cultural embeddedness in everyday practices and language constrains people from imagining alternative arrangements. The impact that globalisation has on knowledge and its sources and innovation expansion was mentioned earlier. Within the literature, the highlight is on how globalisation and national culture exert influence on R&D performance. For example, any company should consider the national/regional milieu when they want to innovate. Thus, the milieu should be favourable to innovation because in some cases when a national/ regional culture is undermined, innovations can be rejected regardless of the amount of resources spent for innovations are high (Jones and Davis, 2000). To date, there is no common and precise definition of culture, thus making it difficult to examine it in relation to innovation (McGrath et al., 1992). Nevertheless, the role of culture is to diffuse, activate, and select among available representations when it is helped by institutions, networks and social movements (DiMaggio, 1997: 263). Thus, scholars highlight the need to understand and to develop the idea of culture, as an interaction of shared cognitive structure and supra-individual cultural phenomena, in the form of media messages, conversations or material culture that activate the cognitive structures (DiMaggio, 1997: 264).

Considering all above-mentioned, we can argue that the interplay between institutions, networks, and cognitive frames form a given field, in which the innovation processes take place. As mentioned earlier, this theoretical understanding can set a new approach toward understanding new economic realities and all development processes that occur in a given field. This theory allows us to provide comprehensive in-depth knowledge about all relevant aspects of the innovation and high-performance computing (HPC) landscape in each of the three pilot regions.

4. Data and Methodology

The need for the operationalisation of the individual elements of innovation systems and factors that determine them has been on the agenda for more than a decade (Balzat and Hanusch, 2004). The variety of explanations of Innovation Systems on different levels is a necessary stage in embedding the topic in a framework, which would allow having a comparable model for operationalisation of the concept of innovation. At present, a number of reports (World Competitiveness Yearbook; Global Competitiveness Report, Innovation Union Scoreboard, Regional Innovation Scoreboard, etc.) deal with innovation on different levels. As we can see, these reports capture both quantitative and qualitative concepts that measure the competitiveness relying on a wide range of indicators. We do not question these approaches and their reliability toward measuring the innovation performance. The embedment of the Social Field Theory in the context of Innovation Systems would offer various possibilities of applying a more coherent operationalisation toward the explanation of innovations as an outcome. Additionally, it would solve the difficulty of focusing on larger number of indicators that sometimes are hard to access.

The approach toward explaining innovation processes with the help of the Social Fields Theory is rather novel. Rončević and Modic (2011) were able to combine the theoretical framework of Social Fields and verify it empirically Qualitative Comparative Analysis. This method was developed by Ragin (1987, 2000, 2008) and enables testing the necessary, and sufficient conditions for any particular outcome. Consequently, in the following period, there were several attempts to combine SOFIA and Qualitative Comparative Analysis (Cepoi and Golob, 2017; Cepoi and Rončević, 2015; Fric and Rončević, 2018). Nonetheless, none of this research has focused on assessing the innovation process and social fields theory with the help of a qualitative approach. Thus, the present paper addresses the absence of a qualitative approach. To collect the data, we conducted two semi-structured interviews with relevant stakeholders from government institutions, businesses, and academia involved in innovation processes in the selected regions (countries). The obtained information was analysed in-depth with the help of the Atlas.ti Qualitative Data Analysis & Research Software.

Additionally, the participants (stakeholders from state agencies, business and academia who deal with innovation processes) had to score (from 1 – very bad to 4 – very good) the issues emphasised during the interviews.

5. The Case of South-East Ireland

Being a strong innovator would indicate having a different innovation system than other regions, or at least to have other determinants and other social realities that impact the regional innovation performance. Following this line of argument, the discussions with the stakeholders from the South-East Ireland highlighted a more complex model of how do the social forces construct the innovation social field. Therefore, the discussions accommodate 12 main points: infrastructure strength, SMEs strength, authorities' strength, human resources strength, competition, cluster strength, culture, authorities' weakness, culture weakness, SMEs weakness, networks, research institution cooperation, SMEs cooperation and trust. As in the case of the previous regions, the focus is on presenting both a general and detailed picture of the status-quo of the innovation performance within the South-East region.

One of the key understandings of the innovation social field is to acknowledge the influence (either positive or negative) of public authorities. One of the aspects is the ***infrastructure,*** more specifically its strengths and weaknesses. The positive aspect of the region is the presence of ***good infrastructure***. The presence of good infrastructure, e.g. ***the interconnectivity of roads***, is associated with abundant job opportunities. Additionally, it can be argued that job opportunities are a result of the fact that the region is characterised by a ***great mix of multinational corporations***. This aspect is regarded as a strength of the public authorities, due to their capabilities to attract these companies, but also a strength of the companies. We will focus on the latter in the following paragraphs. As so, the authorities created a positive premise for the development of the human assets. More explicitly, the presence of a ***highly-skilled work force*** is linked to the ***quality of graduates*** in the region.

Firstly, it was stressed that the ***educational perspective is important,*** which is associated with the fact that the government ***supports*** and ***invests in education.*** Additionally, when the more educated and skilled is the population, than it is an ***attraction*** for companies, especially for the ones that operate abroad. Secondly, in terms of education skills, the role of the authorities again is at the forefront. Consequently, participants pointed out that the authorities are involved and guide the ***setup of institutes*** that produce highly skilled ***graduates***. Even more, this is also associated with setting a good foundation for good institutes and with a ***high-tech software industry***, which is a leader in innovation performance within the South-East region. As a result, these aspects are part of a larger understanding why this region has the capacity to attract talented people. The participants also highlighted the presence of a good ***working environment*** (e.g., job opportunities for both ***local graduates and those from outside the region***), ***international recruits*** and ***local environment***, which ultimately depend directly or indirectly on the authorities. Furthermore, the authorities create ***investments opportunities***. This is a ***good driver for outside interaction***. Additionally, these two are associated with how ***communities are connected with the outside of the region***, which also plays a vital role.

As mentioned earlier, even with the creation of investment opportunities, the main concern of stakeholders regarding the role of the authorities is that institutions have set up an ***environment with no innovative thinking***, which ***is discouraging for new start-ups***. As a result, ***innovation is also discouraged*** because of the '***poor mentality of the local government***' and ***future development is hindered***.

Another aspect is the ***shortage of skills***, which makes it difficult to find key people, especially those with ***science and engineering degrees***. Essentially, the authorities lack the capacity to bridge the ***existent opportunities and the skill needs***. There is also a ***shortage of R&D in the industry***. Additionally, in terms of ***innovation policy***, the stakeholders mentioned ***limited public resources for initiatives***. Overall, even if the authorities ***are trying to do something***, the ***direction is perceived as being wrong***. Therefore, this means that there is ***still a lot of work to do*** to improve the level of development and innovation performance.

Moreover, the role of companies is also important. Companies help the region in several ways. Firstly, enterprises attract innovators by promoting talented people and encouraging remote work. Secondly, through the presence of a good ***quality of life*** that the region offers, ***enterprises can promote the region***. More explicit, the two aspects are good means of region promotion.

During the discussions, stakeholders pointed out that ***companies have great capabilities,*** and they are considered the drivers of innovation. Firstly, the analysis pointed that companies in the South-East region ***understand the needs of the market***. Additionally, the semi-structured interview revealed that ***companies focus on opportunities***, and by doing this, they ***embrace new technologies***. Even so, it is not enough to have the newest technology, but the idea is also to ***focus on the skills of employees and to train the staff***. Secondly, the stakeholders pointed that the region is characterised by a ***high mix of multinational companies***. The presence of multinational companies strengthens the position of outside regional collaboration, in the sense that their presence is associated with the ***focus on the export***. Another strength of the enterprises in the region is that SMEs are ***willing to participate in post-production development***. Even if these are ***part of a chain***, the companies also want to focus on other processes in order to diversify the final products.

Even though the region is an innovation leader, the stakeholders also highlighted some weaknesses of enterprises. One of the main issues pointed out within the discussions is that companies in the region, especially the ***multinationals, do not have R&D activities***. In contrast, when it comes to ***smaller enterprises***, these are doing some but not a lot of ***research and development***. Additionally, the industry and the multinational companies do not deal with R&D. Stakeholders mentioned that in terms of innovation performance, there is a gap between the academic and industrial innovation. Hence, there is a need for the improvement of ***collaborative R&D***. A possible explanation for the fact that multinational companies do not focus much on R&D is that the region has too many sister companies. These companies have close affiliations with other companies and are subsidiaries of a larger, parent enterprise. As a result, smaller companies face ***competition from sister companies,*** which encourages them to focus more on the R&D. Additionally, the stakeholders emphasised that companies have a ***lack of understanding*** (do not collaborate) not only between the ***companies*** that are present in the region. Nevertheless, the lack of understanding with other companies triggers communication with ***education institutions***.

Another aspect of the status quo in terms of how the social forces act was the importance of networks and collaboration, which are important promoters of innovation performance. To have a clearer vision of how these operate, we can highlight that networks and collaborations are organised in several layers. Firstly, there are the networks created between companies. The region has a strong ***cluster of foreign companies***, which is associated with the fact that there is a regional ***focus on the development of clusters***. These clusters allow companies to interact with each other and contribute to the development of the innovative potential of the region. This enables a ***community that has connections outside the region***. All these allow both national and foreign companies to have good ***cooperation*** and ***strong links*** between them. The presence of strong links and cooperation allows the possibility of ***transferability*** of different resources such as ***innovation, knowledge,*** and ***human resources***. Furthermore, the analysis stressed that companies also ***collaborate with educational institutions***. One of the main aims of these collaborations is to focus bridge the skills gap in order to recruit trained and highly skilled employees. Therefore, it would be easier to train them for the needs of the market. Enterprises are ***investing in graduates*** by ***creating innovation partnerships***. This means that companies cooperate with research institutions, while ***research centres collaborate*** between themselves. If there were be a push ***for the idea of collaboration*** and of the ***awareness of the need for collaboration***, the collaboration between centres would be very hard to accomplish. At the same time, there are two main causes why people realised the need for collaboration. Participants mentioned the presence of ***non-competitive basis***, and that people ***do not fear competition anymore.*** Competition is seen as a ***positive*** stimulus for the ***diversification of collaborations***.

Nevertheless, these are not the only factors that determine the awareness of collaborations. Within the region, people are aware ***that there is a need for interaction***. Even more, interaction does not come alone, as people realised the ***importance of sharing***. That is why for example they use ***events as an opportunity for sharing relevant information. This*** would ***not*** be possible if people would ***fight for the same 'piece of pie'.*** Also, one of the main pillars of collaborations is trust. The participants highlighted that ***trust*** is based on ***common goals*** and underlined the fact that ***people trust people, not institutions.*** Stakeholders pointed out that ***people are key actors for successful networks*** because the ***networks are specific***. They rely on the trust of people, and thus the ***trust*** is ***rewarding*** in creating various collaborations. As a result, networks are a means of ***information dissemination***.

Innovation networks in the South-East region are more personality-based and less process-based. Therefore, ***networks bring companies together***, but the ***communication between enterprises and other actors is not good enough***. If the specific context determines ***authorities and companies to cooperate***, it enables an entrepreneurial milieu that attracts foreign investments in the region. The ***economic crisis*** had a vital role: it was a ***catalyst for collaboration processes*** in the region. The recession encouraged ***people to engage more in entrepreneurship*** and to become ***more willing to take risks***. The ***development of new products is seen as a fight against the effects of the recession***.

In contrast, there are also instances when collaborations with the state do not bring the desired outcomes. For example, in academia, most of the networking is project-based and relies on informal networks. The people who participate in a specific project organise these networks. If the state becomes a 'broker', these networks tend to be less successful. Therefore, at this point, we can talk about an industry-specific higher education institution network but not about a sector network.

Nonetheless, the role of culture also has to be considered when it comes to certain habits of the population, such as the cultural resistance towards innovation. Therefore, the population has to understand that 'innovation is an opportunity, not a cost'. Such understanding can influence the realisation of human dignity of individuals (Kleindienst, 2017; Kleindienst and Tomšič, 2017; Kleindienst and Tomšič, 2018; Kleindienst, 2019). Until recently, creativity was limited by mundane jobs, but this is changing. Thanks to foreign cultural influence, the young generation wants to try new things, and people have become internationally focused, which means that they are exposed to positive environments (Golob and Makarovič, 2018; Golob, 2020). At this stage, the participants pointed out the importance of entrepreneurial and collaboration skills and how good assimilation levels help people adapt to new challenges. Also, because necessity is a driver for innovation, it can trigger innovation to become part of people's mindset.

The semi-structured interview and the in-depth analysis in Waterford with the stakeholders have emphasised several essential aspects in terms of how the social field of innovation operates in the context of the three social forces. Each of these families include a number of codes that are interconnected with different types of relations. Additionally, these interconnections show the interplay of the social forces in the context of the Regional Innovation Systems and show how these contribute to the innovation performance

5.1. The Case of South-East Slovenia

The discussion with the stakeholders from the region pointed that it is successful because of its innovativeness. The participants mentioned that there is a regional development programme, which has guidelines for research and innovation. Additionally, Novo mesto is a good place that can attract and retain people with job positions and competitive salaries. Additionally, the region offers a good quality of life, safety and good connections with other cities, but not via public transportation. Private transportation is preferred because public transportation is not well developed.

Within the region, several *big companies* in the automotive and pharmaceutical sectors are active. The presence of important sectors within the region results in high value-added. Therefore, the presence of large companies in the region makes it *exported oriented*. Companies assist the state with financial resources, which creates a good premise for government-business cooperation. Nevertheless, the presence of *different industries* within the region, *industry-institution collaboration* and *trust* contribute to the success of the innovation performance, although it does not go beyond the region.

In contrast, the relationship with business is more complex, but it does not hinder the importance. Previously, emphasis was on the regional *Chamber of Commerce*, an institution that plays a vital role in representing the national authorities for the innovation performance. The regional chamber collaborates with the national chamber of Commerce on various projects at regional and extra-regional levels. Following this line of argument, the chamber offers an environment in which companies can develop and boost the innovation performance in the region. Therefore, the chamber offers tenders for innovation and increases the visibility of innovation by offering basic public information. The stakeholders mentioned that the chamber has a good model for promoting innovation, which makes people more aware of the importance of innovations have in their daily lives. As the participants pointed out, another strong point of the region is that there is a *business incubator*, which offers support and national financing for various enterprises.

Moreover, the performance of authorities also relies on the relationship with academia and businesses. As the participants mentioned, in the past there was an intensive focus on *study programmes*. Public authorities and academia created the necessary conditions for the development and establishment of *faculties according to the needs of the region, and prepared new programmes*, based which on faculties have at their disposal a High-Performance Computer, which can be used for advanced research but also can contribute to the development of innovative products.

However, at the sub-region level, policies regarding the human capital are not performing to the maximum capacity, because the population is not growing very fast. This creates two other problems. First, the region is characterised by the presence of over-educated people but at the same time there is a *lack of engineers*.

Second, there are not enough people dealing with innovation. To solve this issue, stakeholders focus on people from abroad that are culturally compatible. At the same time, even if the authorities created good conditions for many institutions that support innovations, the problem is that these institutions are *not innovators*.

Additionally, the region is characterised by the absence of the institutes, which is associated with the absence of research and development capabilities. One of the explanations is that private entities (e.g., private faculties) *cannot apply for national public tenders*. Moreover, the participants pointed that because the authorities tend to centralise things (to have everything in the *capital*), there are *no long-established universities* in the region. The government is also not thinking of developing any laboratories in the region. Following this line of argument, the interviewees pointed out that the authorities do not listen to the recommendations that come from the region. Therefore, the region is not seen as a partner. At this stage, the region is not a priority; thus, the *collaboration* of enterprises with *the government is not good*.

Even more, further difficulties arise when preparing patent documentation, which highlights the *bureaucracy for innovation protection*. As a result, the stakeholders emphasised the presence of a big administration:

The centralisation not only refers to the academic sphere, but also to the centralisation of financing. The idea is that all the programmes are merged in the national programme. Additionally, the participants pointed that *not having a systematic financing* also hinders the development of the region. Even so, not all the financing is freely available, and it takes effort to collect the necessary information. Additionally, the lack of financial resources causes *difficulties for smaller companies* in terms of *financing*.

As it was mentioned in the previous chapter, there is a regional development programme, but as the participants pointed out, there is no innovation policy.

Therefore, the absence of an innovation policy is the cause why there is no big impact in terms of innovation performance.

As the participants described, the overall situation is that within the region there are bad conditions for development, especially for SMEs. As the stakeholders mentioned, the region does not have an insight into small companies. Nevertheless, the authorities' lack of insight regarding small enterprises within the region does not impact how the business milieu interacts. Following this line of argument, big companies have departments for R&D. Additionally, these companies have resources to invest (including their own knowledge) and achieve good results. Large enterprises have the capacity to support innovation, which means that the region depends on them in terms of innovation development. Another aspect is that these big companies in the region do not see each other as competitors, which enables information sharing between them. The *good relationship at the industrial level* is comprehended as a suitable relation model, because it focuses on different networks. Hence, the industry *collaborates with small enterprises* and attempt to innovate or to have *company-institute cooperation*, because cooperation is perceived as *a need* in the region. Good collaborations are associated with the presence of academics in entrepreneurship, as lecturing for companies is one of the ways through which this relationship is consolidated.

However, the presence of big companies in the region is only one side of the story. The second part refers to small enterprises and the problems they face in the region. Innovation in the region is dependent on the large companies and their funding. The region is characterised by a small number of SMEs that contribute to the not-so-big entrepreneurial experience in the region. Therefore, the problems of financing small companies are associated with the fact that they *do not have R&D capacities and departments*. Furthermore, the relationship between SMEs and government is not as good as it could be. This relationship is characterised by not having a good link between the two and being seen as a one-sided connection.

Even if the information (funding opportunities, seminars, etc.) is available at the Regional Chamber of Commerce, enterprises do not search there for information and prefer to rely on their sources, even though it *takes some effort to gather the relevant information*. At the same time, SMEs have problems with patent applications. The *bureaucracy for innovation protection* creates *difficulties in preparing the necessary documentation*. Additionally, it is expensive for SMEs to protect their intellectual property and many of them try to cover the costs, which in the case of the SMEs are high. Even more, they cover it because the technologies are developing fast or because these companies are part of a supply chain, and the patent can disclose their idea. Therefore, if innovation is actually happening, then there are high chances that these will not be reported.

Within the region, the environment is limited to the IT industry, which means that most companies are not competitors. This can have negative effects, such as determining these companies not to seek constant improvement and become non-innovators. As the participants pointed out, competition is crucial to the process of innovation and regional development.

The presence of different faculties in the region constitutes a strong point for the region, whose *education* programmes constitute a point of attraction. However, the participants pointed out that the best students leave for the capital. Through their research institutes, these faculties used to be the main contributors to patent filings because most of the research and development in the region was done by universities and research institutes. However, those patents were not financially successful and, as a result, there is *not much research and development* left. That is also accompanied by the *lack of institutes.*

To date, the emphasis was on the interconnection between public institutions, businesses and academia. As the participants highlighted during the semi-structured interview, the cognitive aspect of the region is also at forefront in explaining people's attitudes toward development. People have strong ideas, and thus they are creative. As the participants pointed out, critical thinking is even more important. Additionally, they prefer to work, and in most cases, they have a second job. In many cases, the extra job stimulates the spread of the grey economy in the region. In terms of entrepreneurship, people would prefer a stable job, instead of starting/ becoming an entrepreneur.

At the same time, the participants pointed out that technology implementation leads to the creation of a supportive environment. Furthermore, the presence of innovation is a key driver of the global market, where stakeholders face a better competition. Globalisation offers a bigger access to knowledge, where you have to be innovative in order to be successful.

6. Conclusions

Economic models are simpler if the non-economic aspects are not considered, but, by doing so, it might affect the costs of the available technologies for the economic action. Therefore, it is risky to predict the goal by excluding the social phenomena. Nevertheless, when social phenomena are considered, it aims to make norms, history, institutions, networks or culture, endogenous to economic models. As a result, this will imply that no systematic argument can be made (Granovetter, 2005: 47). The proposed approach can address the social complexity of innovation processes within different regions (Gangaliuc, 2019), which will enable having a universal approach regardless of the regional innovation development level. More explicitly, the tool did not only aim to describe how regions perform in terms of innovation but also to point the strong and weak points of the regional characteristics from the standpoint of SOFIA. Additionally, alongside the theoretical framework, the aim was to demonstrate that the interactions of the actors are embedded in any social field of innovation relying on the three social forces.

The theoretical considerations were backed by the proposed model, where the three social forces contribute to the appearance and development of innovations and contribute to development performance within the two regions. These insights can be considered for policy recommendations for developing the innovative capacity of the two regions. Nevertheless, the SOFIA tool has to be tested in more regions; thus, it will enrich the literature and bring new insights into this approach.

References

Aarikka-Stenroos, L., Sandberg, B. and Lehtimäki, T. (2014). Networks for the Commercialization of Innovations: A Review of How Divergent Network Actors Contribute. *Science Direct*, 43 (3): 365–381. https://doi.org/10.1016/j.indmarman.2013.12.005

Adam, F., Makarovič, M., Rončević, B. and Tomšič, M. (2005). *The Challenges of Sustained Development: The Role of Socio-cultural Factors in East-Central Europe*. New York; Budapest: Central European University Press.

Adams, M. (2006). Hybridizing Habitus and Reflexivity: Towards an Understanding of Contemporary Identity? *Sociology*, 40 (3): 511–528.

Ahrweiler, P. and Keane, M. (2013). Innovation networks. *Mind and Society*, 12: 73–90, DOI: 10.1007/s11299-013-0123-7.

Beckert, J. (2010). How Do Fields Change? The Interrelations of Institutions, Networks, and Cognition in the Dynamics of Markets. *Organization Studies*, 31(5): 605–627.

Besednjak Valič, T., Kolar, J., and Lamut, U. (2020). Three Scenarios of Innovation and Technology Transfer: The Case of Key Enabling Technologies in the Danube Region. *Journal of Engineering and Applied Sciences*, 15: 3619–3623.

Cepoi, V., and Golob, T. (2017). Innovation Performance in the EU Comparative Perspective: The Interplay of Social Forces in the Context of National Innovation Systems. *Comparative Sociology*, 16(4): 555–579.

Cepoi, V., and Rončević, B. (2015). Social Fields Theory Explaining Innovations and Developmental Performance. *4th International Conference on Economics, Political and Law Sciences* (Business and economic series), 38 – 47.

DiMaggio, P. (1997). Culture and Cognition. *Annual Review of Sociology*, 23(1): 263–287.

Fligstein, N. (2001). Social Skill and the Theory of Fields. *Sociological Theory,* 19(2): 105–125.

Fric, U. (2019). Impact of Circular Economy as the EU's Ambitious Policy. *Research in Social Change*, 11 (2): 79 – 96. DOI:10.2478/rsc-2019-0010.

Fric, U., and Roncevic, B. (2018). E-simbioza: Leading a Way to a Circular Economy through Industrial Symbiosis in Slovenia. *Socijalna ekologija: časopis za ekološku misao i sociologijska istraživanja okoline*, 27(2): 119–140.

Fukugawa, N. (2006). Science Parks in Japan and Their Value-Added Contributions to New Technology-Based Firms. *International Journal of Industrial Organization*, 24(2): 381–400.

Gangaliuc, C. (2019). The Measurement of Innovation for Management, Research and Policy. *Research in Social Change*, 11(2): 35–57. DOI:10.2478/rsc-2019-0008.

Golob, T. (2020). Notranji dialog, refleksivnost in odgovorno delovanje mladih = Internal dialogue, reflexivity, and responsible behavior of the young, *Phainomena: [glasilo Fenomenološkega društva v Ljubljani]*, 29(114/115): 193–222, DOI: 10.32022/PHI29.2020.114-115.9.

Golob, T., and Makarovič, M. (2017). Self-organisation and Development: A Comparative Approach to Post-Communist Transformations from the Perspective of Social Systems Theory. *Europe-Asia studies,* 69(10): 1499–1525.

Golob, T., and Makarovič, M. (2018). Student Mobility and Transnational Social Ties as Factors of Reflexivity. *Social Sciences,* 7(3): 1–18.

Granovetter, M. (2005). The Impact of Social Structure on Economic Outcomes. *The Journal of Economic Perspectives,* 19(1): 33–50.

Jakobsen, S.-E., and Aarset B. (2010). Institutions as Facilities for Change? A Study of the Coherence between Political Regulations and Innovations within the Pelagic Fisheries Sector in Norway. *Marine Policy,* 34: 928–934.

Jones, G. K., and Davis Herber, J. (2000). National Culture and Innovation: Implications for Locating Global R&D Operations. MIR: *Management International Review,* 40(1): 11–39.

Kleindienst, P. (2017). Understanding the Different Dimensions of Human Dignity: Analysis of the Decision of the Constitutional Court of the Republic of Slovenia on the "Tito Street" Case, *DANUBE: Law and Economics Review,* 8/3, 117–137, DOI: 10.1515/danb-2017-0009.

Kleindienst, P. (2019). Zgodovinski temelji sodobne paradigme človekovega dostojanstva. *Phainomena* 28(108–109): 259–282, DOI: 10.32022/PHI28.2019.108-109.11.

Kleindienst, P., and Tomšič, M. (2017). Human Dignity as the Foundation of Democratic Political Culture: Legal and Philosophical Perspective. *Law, Culture and the Humanities,* 1–20, DOI: 10.177/143872117738229.

Kleindienst, P., and Tomšič, M. (2018). Človekovo dostojanstvo kot del politične culture v novih demokracijah: postkomunistična Slovenija. *Bogoslovni vestnik,* 78(1): 159–172.

Kolleck, N. (2013). Social Network Analysis in Innovation Research: Using a Mixed Methods Approach to Analyze Social Innovations. *European Journal of Futures Research,* 15(25), DOI: 10.1007/s40309-013-0025-2.

MacGrath, R., MacMillan, I., Ai-Yuan Yang, E., and Tsai, W. (1992). Does Culture Endure or Is It Malleable? *Journal of Business Venturing,* 7(6): 441–458.

Modic, D., and Rončević, B. (2018). Social Topography for Sustainable Innovation Policy: Putting Institutions, Social Networks and Cognitive Frames in Their Place. *Comparative Sociology,* 17(1): 100–127.

North, D. C. (1990). *Institutions, Institutional Change and Economic Performance.* Cambridge: Cambridge University Press.

Nowacki, R., and Bachnik, K. (2016). Innovations within Knowledge Management. *Journal Business Research,* 69(5): 1577–1581.

Pandiloska Jurak, A. (2020). The Importance of High-Tech Companies for EU Economy: Overview and the EU Grand Strategies Perspective. *Research in Social Change,* 12(3), 32–52. DOI:10.2478/rsc-2020-0013.

Pandiloska Jurak, A., and Pinterič, U. (2012). Assessment of Municipalities' Performances in Slovenia. *Transylvanian review of administrative sciences,* 35: 121–137.

Ragin, C. (2000). *Fuzzy-set Social Science.* Chicago: University of Chicago Press.

Ragin, C. (2008). Measurement versus calibration: A set-theoretic approach. In Box-Steffensmeier, J., Brady, H. and Collier, D. (eds.): *The Oxford Handbook of Political Methodology.* Oxford: Oxford University Press.

Rončević, B. (2012). Regional development agencies and changing social fields: Towards a sociology of regional systems of innovation. In: Bellini, N., Danson, M. and Halkier, H. (eds.) *Regional Development Agencies: The Next Generation?: Networking, Knowledge and Regional Policies.* London; New York: Routledge, 87–101.

Rončević, B. (2019). Cultural Political Economy of Europe 2020: Jean Monnet Chair CPE 2020 and Its Impact. *Research in Social Change*, 11(2), 5–13. DOI: 10.2478/rsc-2019-0006.

Rončević, B. (2020). Technology and Innovations in Regional Development for Europe 2020: Jean Monnet Centre of Excellence TIR 2020 for Smart, Inclusive and Sustainable Growth. *Research in Social Change*, 12(3): 5–14. DOI: 10.2478/rsc-2020-0011.

Rončević, B., and Besednjak Valič, T. (2019). How to Think about Regional Development Agencies as a Sociologist. *The Social Sciences*, 14(9): 326–334.

Rončević, B., Makarovič, M., Tomšič, M., and Cepoi, V. (2018). Methodological solutions for comparative research on transformations. In: Vihalemm, P., Masso, A., Opermann, S. (eds.) *The Routledge International Handbook of European Social Transformations*. London and New York: Routledge, 57–70.

Rončević, B., and Modic, D. (2011). Regional Systems of Innovations as Social Fields. *Sociologija i prostor: časopis za istraživanje prostornoga i sociokulturnog razvoja*, 49(191): 313–333.

Rončević, B., and Modic, D. (2012). Social fields of technological innovations. In: Genov, N. (ed.) *Global Trends and Regional Development*. New York: Routledge, 226–247.

Rončević, B., Šušteršič, J., Wostner, P., and Besednjak Valič, T. (2010). Quo Vadis, Slovenia? Between Framework Conditions and Internal Capabilities. *Managing Global Transitions*, *8*(4): 353–380.

Rončević, B., and Tomšič, M. (2017). Perspectives of information society: Bricolage of manifestations. In: Rončević, B. and Tomšič, M. (eds.) *Information Society and Its Manifestations: Economy, Politics, Culture*. Frankfurt am Main: Peter Lang, 9–21.

Rosenfeld, R. (1996). A Maximum Entropy Approach to Adaptive Statistical Language Modelling. *Computer, Speech and Language*, 10(3): 187–228.

Tomšič, M. and Kleindienst, P. (2017). E-Participation, e-democracy and political engagement of the citizenry in Central and Eastern Europe. In: Rončević, B., and Tomšič, M. (eds.) *Information Society and Its Manifestations: Economy, Politics, Culture*. Frankfurt am Main. [etc.]: PL Academic Research. DOI: 10.3726/b10694.

Keywords Index

Authors' Index